DICTIONARY OF
DEMOGRAPHY

DICTIONARY OF DEMOGRAPHY

MULTILINGUAL GLOSSARY

WILLIAM PETERSEN
AND
RENEE PETERSEN

with the collaboration of an
International Panel of Demographers

GREENWOOD PRESS
Westport, Connecticut • London, England

Library of Congress Cataloging in Publication Data

Petersen, William.
  Dictionary of demography.

    1. Demography—Dictionaries—Polyglot. 2. Popu-
lation—Dictionaries—Polyglot. 3. Dictionaries,
Polyglot. I. Petersen, Renee. II. Title.
HB849.2.P468 1985   304.6′03   85-27055
ISBN 0-313-25139-8 (lib. bdg. : alk. paper)

Library of Congress Catalog Card Number: 85-27055
ISBN: 0-313-25139-8

First published in 1985

Greenwood Press
A division of Congressional Information Service, Inc.
88 Post Road West
Westport, Connecticut 06881

Printed in the United States of America

The paper used in this book complies with the
Permanent Paper Standard issued by the National
Information Standards Organization (Z39.48-1984).

10 9 8 7 6 5 4 3 2 1

Contents

Introduction

The glossary begins with a translation from English into each of the world's principal research languages. The order of these languages is arbitrary, set by convenience in pagination: French, Spanish, Italian, and German in the first batch; Japanese and Chinese in the second batch; and Russian in the third. The translations from each of these languages into English follow the same order. When a word in any other language differs in grammatical form from the English, it is marked with adj. for adjective, f. for female or feminine, m. for male or masculine, n. for noun, pl. for plural, or v. for verb.

Often alternative designations with more or less the same meaning are given in some of the languages, but usually not in all of them. The correspondence across the page, thus, is not from one word to another but from one grouping to another. In each case the order of these approximate synonyms is with the standard term first, followed by less common or colloquial words or phrases. In order to distinguish such alternatives, phrases too long to be printed in one line have the second line indented. Alternatives are printed flush except in the English list, where they are indented in order to maintain the alphabetical sequence of the standard terms.

MULTILINGUAL
GLOSSARY

English to French, Spanish, Italian, and German

English	French
abortion	avortement
abortion, induced	avortement provoqué interruption (volontaire) de grossesse
abortion, spontaneous miscarriage	avortement spontané fausse couche
acculturation	acculturation
accuracy	précision
adolescence	adolescence
adolescent, n.	adolescent, m. jeunes gens, pl.
adult, n.	adulte
age	âge
age distribution age structure	composition par âge structure par âge
age group(ing) age bracket	groupe d'âges
age-specific rate	taux par âge taux selon l'âge atteint taux de génération
agglomeration. *See* standard metropolitan area.	
aging, n.	vieillissement (démographique)
alien, n.	étranger, m.
analysis	analyse

area
  territory
  region
	territoire
	division territoriale
	région

Spanish	Italian	German
aborto	aborto interruzione della gravidanza	Fehlgeburt Abortus Abort
aborto provocado	aborto provocato aborto procurato	künstliche Schwangerschaftsun- terbrechung Schwangerschaftsabbruch künstlicher Abort
aborto espontáneo malparto pérdido	aborto involontario aborto spontaneo	Spontanabortus Fruchtabgang
adaptación cultural	adattamento culturale	kulturelle Anpassung
exactitud precisión	precisione accuratezza	Genauigkeit
adolescencia	adolescenza	Jugendalter jugentliches Alter
adolescente	adolescente	Jüngling, m. junges Mädchen, f. Jugendlicher, m.
adulto, m.	adulto, m.	Erwachsener, m.
edad	età	Alter
distribución por edad composición por edad estructura por edad	distribuzione per età struttura per età composizione per età	Altersaufbau Altersgliederung Altersverteilung Altersstruktur
grupo etario grupo de edades intervalo de edades	gruppo secondo l'età classe pluriennale d'età classe poliennale d'età	Altersgruppe
tasa por edades	tasso secondo l'età quoziente specifico per età	altersspezifische Rate altersspezifische Ziffer
envejecimiento	invecchiamento	Alterung Überalterung
extranjero, m.	straniero, m. forestiero, m.	Ausländer, m.
análisis estudio	analisi	Analyse
área territorio región zona superficie	area territorio regione	Gebiet Raum Region

English	French
arrival (of immigrants)	arrivée
assimilation	assimilation
attribute. *See* characteristic.	
average. *See* mean, adj.; mean, n.	
baby. *See* infant.	
bachelor	célibataire du sexe masculin
base, n.	base
birth	naissance accouchement
birth control	prévention des naissances limitation des naissances restriction des naissances contrôle des naissances
birth interval	intervalle génésique
birth, live	naissance vivante
birth, multiple	accouchement multiple accouchement gémellaire
birth order. *See* parity.	
birth, premature	accouchement prématuré accouchement avant terme
birth rate	taux de natalité
block, n.	îlot
boarder lodger	pensionnaire locataire d'une chambre meublée
bunching. *See* heaping.	
capital (city)	capitale
celibacy	célibat

Spanish	Italian	German
entrada	arrivo entrata ingresso	Zuzug Ankunft Zuwanderung Einwanderung
asimilación	assimilazione	Assimilation Eingliederung
soltero	celibe	Junggeselle
base	base	Basis Basisgrösse Basiszahl
nacimiento	nascita	Geburt
control de la natalidad regulación de los nacimientos restricción de los nacimientos control de los nacimientos	regolazione delle nascite controllo delle nascite regolamentazione delle nascite	Geburtenbeschränkung Geburtenkontrolle
intervalo genésico	intervallo genesico intervallo tra nascite	Geburtenabstand
nacido vivo, m. nacimiento de niño vivo, m.	nato vivo, m. nascita di un nato vivo, m.	Lebendgeburt
nacimiento múltiple alumbramiento múltiple	parto plurimo parto multiplo	Mehrlingsgeburt
nacimiento prematuro alumbramiento prematuro	parto prematuro nascita prematura parto avanti termine	verfrühte Geburt Frühgeburt
tasa de natalidad	quoziente di natalità quoziente generico di natalità quoziente di natalità (generale)	Geburtenrate Geborenenziffer Geburtenziffer
manzana	isolato caseggiato	Block Häuserblock
huésped pensionista	pensionante dozzinante inquilino, m. locatario di camera ammobiliata, m.	Pensionsgast Untermieter
capital	capitale	Hauptstadt
celibato	celibato (of males) nubilato (of females)	Ehelosigkeit

7

English	French
census	recensement dénombrement
census tract	secteur de dépouillement district de recensement
central city	noyau urbain
cervical cap. *See* diaphragm.	
chance. *See* risk.	
characteristic attribute	caractère qualitatif
child-woman ratio	rapport enfants-femmes
citizen	citoyen, m.
city town	ville
civil status. *See* marital status.	
classify	classer ventiler
climacteric. *See* menopause.	
code, v.	chiffrer
cohabitation. *See* coitus.	
cohort	cohorte génération promotion
cohort fertility. *See* fertility, cohort.	
cohort, synthetic	génération hypothétique génération fictive cohorte fictive
coitus sexual intercourse cohabitation	coït rapport sexuel
coitus interruptus withdrawal	coït interrompu méthode de retrait
color (of skin)	couleur

Spanish	Italian	German
censo empadronamiento	censimento	Volkszählung
sector censal	sezione di censimento circoscrizione comunale	Zählbezirk
núcleo urbano	centro urbano nucleo urbano	Stadtkern
característica atributo	carattere qualitativo carattere mutabile	(qualitatives) Merkmal (artmässiges) Merkmal Eigenschaft Kennzeichen
relación niños-mujeres	rapporto bambini-donne rapporto tra figli e donne	Kinder-Frauenziffer
ciudadano, m.	cittadino, m.	Staatsangehöriger, m. Staatsbürger, m.
ciudad pueblo villa	città	Grosstadt Stadt
clasificar	classificare	gruppieren klassifizieren
codificar	codificare	signieren
cohorte	coorte generazione	Kohorte Jahrgang
cohorte hipotética generación ficticia	coorte fittizia generazione fittizia coorte sintetica generazione ipotetica	fiktive Generation
coito relaciones sexuales	coito rapporto sessuale coabitazione	Geschlechtsverkehr Beischlaf Koitus Kohabitation
coito interrumpido	coito interrotto	coitus interruptus unterbrochener Beischlaf
color	colore	Hautfarbe

English	French
commuter	navetteur, m.
commuting, n.	navette
	migration alternante
computer (electronic)	machine électronique
conception	conception
concubinage. *See* union.	
condom	préservatif (masculin)
sheath	condom
conjugal status. *See* marital status.	
contraception	contraception
contraceptive, n.	(matériel) contraceptif
contraceptive method	méthode contraceptive
	méthode anticonceptionelle
contraceptive, oral	contraceptif oral
contraceptive pill	pilule contraceptive
contraceptive, postcoital	contraception postcoïtale
morning-after pill	pilule du lendemain
conurbation. *See* standard metropolitan area.	
corrected. *See* revised.	
count, n.	comptage
country	pays
couple (married)	couple marié
cross-tabulation. *See* tabulation, cross.	
crude (of a rate)	brut, m.
data	renseignements numériques
	données numériques

Spanish	Italian	German
trabajador conmutante, m.*	viaggiatore giornaliero	Pendler, m.
	andare e venire movimenti a spola spostamenti pendolari	Pendelwanderung
computadora electrónica	calcolatore elettronico	(elektronische) Grossrechenan- lage
concepción	concepimento	Empfängnis Konzeption
preservativo condón	preservativo profilattico	Präservativ
anticoncepción	controllo delle nascite contraccettività	Empfängnisverhütung Kontrazeption
anticonceptivo	anticoncezionale mezzo anticoncezionale	kontrazeptives Mittel
método anticonceptivo	metodo di controllo delle nascite metodo anticoncezionale pratica anticoncezionale	empfängnisverhütende Methode kontrazeptive Methode antikonzeptionelle Methode
anticonceptivo oral	contraccettivo orale	orales Kontrazeptivum
pildora anticonceptiva	pillola contraccettiva	kontrazeptive Pille
anticonceptivo post coito	contraccettivo postcoitale contraccettivo successivo al coito contraccettivo successivo al rap- porto	"Pille danach"
recuento enumeración	calcolo conteggio	Auszählung
país	paese	Land
pareja (matrimonial)	sposi coppia maritata	Ehepaar Paar
bruta, f. cruda, f.	greggio, m. grezzo, m.	roh
datos	dati	Angaben Daten

*Translates the English, but not a usual term.

11

English	French
data, basic	données de base
crude data	données brutes
primary data	
raw data	
death	décès
	mort, n.
death, cause of	cause de décès
death certificate	bulletin de décès
death, probability of	quotient de mortalité
death rate	taux de mortalité
demographer	démographe
demographic transition	révolution vitale
demographic revolution	révolution démographique
vital revolution	transition démographique
demography	démographie
denomination (religious)	culte
departure (of emigrants)	sortie
	départ
dependency ratio	rapport de dépendance
dependent, n.	dépendant, m.
	personne à charge
dependent children	enfants à charge
depopulation	dépopulation
	dépeuplement
diagram	diagramme
graph	graphique
diaphragm	pessaire occlusif
cervical cap	diaphragme (vaginal)
pessary	cape (cervicale)
	préservatif féminin
difference	écart

Spanish	Italian	German
datos básicos	dati fondamentali	Ausgangsdaten
datos brutos	dati grezzi	Rohergebnisse
datos primarios	dati primarii	rohe Daten
datos crudos		
muerte	morte	Sterbefall
fallecimiento	decesso	Tod
defunción		
causa de muerte	causa di morte	Todesursache
certificado de defunción	certificato di morte	Sterbeurkunde
acta de defunción	scheda individuale di morte	
probabilidad de muerte	probabilità di morte	Sterbewahrscheinlichkeit
tasa de mortalidad	quoziente di mortalità	Sterberate
	tasso di mortalità	Sterbeziffer
demógrafo, m.	demografo, m.	Demograph, m.
		Bevölkerungswissenschaftler, m.
transición demográfica	transizione demografica	demographischer Übergang
revolución demográfica	rivoluzione demografica	demographische Revolution
revolución vital		demographische Transformation
demografía	demografia	Demographie
		Bevölkerungswissenschaft
		Bevölkerungslehre
culto	culto	Glaubensgemeinschaft
		Konfession
salida	uscita	Fortzug
	espatrio	Abwanderung
		Auswanderung
razón de dependencia	indice di dipendenza	(demographische) Belastungs-quote
dependiente	persona a carico	Angehöriger, m.
hijos dependientes	figli a carico	unversorgte Kinder
		abhängige Kinder
despoblación	spopolamento	Entvölkerung
	declino demografico	
diagrama	diagramma	Schaubild
gráfico	grafico	Diagram
		Kartogram
diafragma	diaframma	Okklusivpessar
	pessario	Cervix Kappe
		Pessar
diferencia	differenza	Unterschied

disability	incapacité
	déficience
disease	maladie
dispersion	dispersion
scatter, n.	
displaced person	personne déplacée
distribution (frequency)	distribution
divorce	divorce
dwelling unit	logement
residence	
ecology, human	écologie humaine
economic development	(rythme de) développement économique
economic growth	
economic sector. *See* industry.	
education, higher	enseignement supérieur
education, primary	enseignement du premier degré
elementary education	enseignement primaire
education, secondary	enseignement du second degré
	enseignement secondaire
emigration	émigration
employed	ayant un emploi
endogenous (of a death)	(décès) endogène
	(mortalité) endogène
enumeration	énumération
enumerator	recenseur, m.
epidemic, n.	maladie épidémique

Spanish	Italian	German
desviación	errore scarto scostamento	Differenz
incapacidad	inabilità invalidità	Arbeitsunfähigkeit
enfermedad	malattia	Krankheit
dispersión	dispersione variabilità	Dispersion Streuung
persona desplazada	rifugiato, m. profugo, m.	Vertriebener, m. Zwangsumsiedler, m. Aussiedler, m.
distribución	distribuzione	Verteilung Häufigkeitsverteilung
divorcio	divorzio	Ehescheidung Scheidung
vivienda residencia	abitazione residenza dimora	Wohnung Wohnsitz
ecología humana	ecologia umana	soziale Ökologie
desarrollo económico crecimiento económico	sviluppo economico crescita economica	Wirtschaftsentwicklung Wirtschaftswachstum
enseñanza superior	istruzione superiore	Hochschulausbildung
enseñanza primaria	istruzione elementare istruzione primaria	Grundschulausbildung Elementarausbildung
enseñanza secundaria enseñanza media	istruzione secondaria istruzione media	Realschul- und Gymnasialaus- bildung
emigración	emigrazione	Auswanderung
empleado, m.	occupato, m.	erwerbstätig
(causa) endógena	(causa) endogena	endogen
enumeración empadronamiento recuento	enumerazione	Zählung Erhebung
enumerador, m. empadronador, m. agente censal	enumeratore agente di censimento ufficiale di censimento intervisatore	Zähler, m.
epidemia	epidemia malattia epidemica	epidemische Krankheit Seuche Epidemie

English	French
estimate, n. estimation	estimation
estimate, v.	estimer
ethnic group	groupe ethnique
eugenics	eugénisme eugénique
ever married, adj.	non-célibataire
exogenous (of a death)	(décès) exogène (mortalité) exogène
expectation of life. *See* life expectancy.	
extrapolation	extrapolation
family	famille
family allowance family subsidy	allocation familiale
family, nuclear	élément familial principal famille biologique famille conjugale famille nucléaire famille restreinte
family planning	planification de la famille planification des naissances régulation des naissances
family size	dimension de la famille
farm population. *See* population, agricultural.	
fecundability	fécondabilité
fecundity	fertilité
female, n. woman	individu du sexe féminin femme
fertility natality	fécondité natalité
fertility, cohort	fécondité d'une cohorte

16

Spanish	Italian	German
valor estimado estimación	stima valore stimato	Schätzung
estimar calcular	stimare	schätzen
grupo étnico	gruppo etnico	Volksgruppe ethnische Gruppe
eugenesia	eugenica	Eugenik
no soltero, m.	(persona) comunque coniugata non celibe	nicht ledig
(causa) exógena	(causa) esogena	exogen
extrapolación	estrapolazione extrapolazione	Extrapolation
familia	famiglia	Familie
subsidio familiar	sussidio familiare premio familiare assegno familiare	Familienbeihilfe Kinderzulage Kinderbeihilfe Kindergeld
núcleo familiar	nucleo familiare principale famiglia nucleare	Kernfamilie Familienkern
planificación familiar planificación de la familia	pianificazione delle nascite pianificazione della famiglia dimensionamento della famiglia	Geburtenregelung Familienplanung
tamaño de la familia	dimensione della famiglia grandezza della famiglia	Familiengrösse
fecundabilidad	fecondabilità	Empfängnisfähigkeit
fertilidad	fertilità	(physiologische) Fruchtbarkeit
individuo del sexo femenino mujer hembra	femmina donna	Person weiblichen Geschlechts Frau
fecundidad natalidad	fecondità natalità	Fruchtbarkeit Geborenenhäufigkeit Geburtlichkeit Natalität
fecundidad de una cohorte	fecondità di una coorte fecondità di una generazione	Fruchtbarkeit einer Kohorte Fruchtbarkeit eines Jahrgangs

English	French
fertility, completed	descendance finale
	descendance complète
fertility rate	taux de fécondité
fertility rate, total	indice synthétique de fécondité
fertilization	fécondation
fetus	fœtus (or fétus)
figure. See number.	
fluctuation	fluctuation
	variation
	mouvement particulier
follow-up, n.	rappel
foreign-born	né à l'étranger, m.
form, n.	imprimé
generation	génération
generation, length of a	durée moyenne d'une génération
genetics	génétique
geographical distribution	localisation du peuplement
spatial distribution	répartition géographique territoriale
	répartition géographique spatiale
geographical mobility	mobilité
spatial mobility	mobilité spatiale
geometric mean	moyenne géométrique
geriatrics	gériatrie
gerontology	gérontologie
gestation. See pregnancy.	

Spanish	Italian	German
fecundidad final fecundidad completada	fecondità complessiva fecondità finale fecondità totale	endgültige Nachkommenschaft
tasa de fecundidad tasa de natalidad	tasso di fecondità quoziente di fecondità	Fruchtbarkeitsrate Fruchtbarkeitsziffer
tasa global de fecundidad tasa total de fecundidad	tasso totale di fecondità indice cumulativo di fecondità finale	Index der Gesamtfruchtbarkeit Gesamtfruchtbarkeitsrate
fecundación	fecondazione	Befruchtung
feto	feto	Fötus
fluctuación variación	fluttuazione andamento particolare variazione particolare	Schwankung Fluktuation
seguimiento	visita ripetuta* sollecito*	fortlaufende Ergänzung Wiederaufnehmung Vervollständigung Ergänzung
nacido en el extranjero, m.	nato all'estero, m.	im Ausland geboren
formulario	scheda modello modulo stampato	Vordruck Formblatt
generación	generazione	Generation
duración media de una genera- ción	durata media di una generazione intervallo medio fra generazioni successive	(durchschnittliche) Generations- dauer
genética	genetica	Genetik
distribución geográfica distribución espacial distribución territorial	distribuzione geografica distribuzione territoriale distribuzione spaziale	geographische Verteilung räumliche Verteilung
movilidad geográfica movilidad espacial	mobilità territoriale mobilità geografica mobilità spaziale	Wanderung Mobilität geographische Mobilität räumliche Mobilität
media geométrica promedio geométrico	media geometrica	geometrisches Mittel
geriatría	geriatria	Geriatrie
gerontología	gerontologia	Gerontologie

*Neither phrase exactly translates the English. *Visita ripetuta* would ordinarily refer to another house call by a doctor, *sollecito* to a second mailing of a postal questionnaire.

English	French
graph. *See* diagram.	
gross	brut, m.
group	classe
hamlet	hameau
head. *See* household.	
heaping	attraction des nombres ronds
bunching	attraction des âges ronds
heredity	hérédité
household	ménage
household, head of a	chef du ménage
household, member of a	membre du ménage
illegitimacy	illégitimité
illegitimate	illégitime
immigration	immigration
incidence rate	taux de morbidité (incidente)
index	indice
indicator	indice
individual	individu
person	personne
soul	âme
industry	branche d'activité économique
sector of the economy	secteur d'activité économique
infant	enfant en bas âge
baby	bébé
infecundity. *See* sterility.	
inhabitant	habitant, m.
interpolation	interpolation
interviewer	enquêteur

Spanish	Italian	German
bruto, m.	lordo, m.	roh Brutto-
grupo clase agrupamiento	classe gruppo	Gruppe Klasse
caserio	borgo piccolo villaggio rurale	Flecken
atracción a ciertos números	attrazione dei numeri arrotondati tendenza all'arrotondamento	Häufung runder Zahlen Bündeln (von Zahlen)
herencia	ereditarietà eredità	Erblichkeit Vererbung
hogar	famiglia (in senso statistico)	Haushalt
jefe de familia cabeza de familia	capofamiglia	Haushaltsvorstand
miembro familiar	membro della famiglia	Haushaltsmitglied
ilegitimidad	illegittimità	Unehelichkeit
ilegítimo, m.	illegittimo, m.	unehelich
inmigración	immigrazione	Einwanderung
tasa de incidencia tasa de morbilidad	tasso di incidenza quoziente di morbosità	Erkrankungsziffer Morbiditätsziffer Erkrankungshäufigkeit
índice	indice	Index
indicador	indicatore	Indikator
individuo persona alma	individuo persona anima	Individuum Person Seele
rama de actividad económica sector económico	settore di attività economica ramo di attività economica	Wirtschaftsabteilung Wirtschaftssektor Wirtschaftszweig
infante criatura niño pequeño, m.	infante	Säugling Kleinkind Baby
habitante	abitante	Bewohner, m. Einwohner, m.
interpolación	interpolazione	Interpolation
entrevistador, m. visitador, m.	intervistatore	Interviewer, m. Befrager, m.

intra-uterine device IUD	dispositif intra-utérin DIU stérilet
intrinsic rate true rate	taux intrinsèque
IUD. *See* intra-uterine device.	
kin. *See* relatives.	
lactation (prolonged)	allaitement (prolongé)
landlord. *See* owner.	
language, native. *See* mother tongue.	
legitimacy	légitimité
legitimate	légitime
length of life. *See* longevity.	
less developed country underdeveloped country	pays sous-développé pays insuffisament développé
life expectancy expectation of life	espérance de vie
life expectancy at birth mean length of life	espérance de vie à la naissance vie moyenne
life, median length of probable length of life	vie médiane vie probable
life span	longévité
life table mortality table	table de mortalité
life table, abridged	table abrégée de mortalité
life table, complete	table complète de mortalité table de mortalité détaillée
literate person	alphabète
living, level of standard of living	niveau de vie
lodger. *See* boarder.	
longevity length of life	durée de la vie

Spanish	Italian	German
dispositivo intra-uterino DIU	spirale	intra-uterin Pessar
tasa intrinseca tasa real	tasso intrinseco saggio intrinseco saggio vero	stabile Rate wahre Rate reine Rate
lactación (prolongada)	allattamento (prolungato)	Säugen (anhaltendes)
legitimidad	legittimità	Ehelichkeit
legítimo, m.	legittimo, m.	ehelich
país en desarrollo país subdesarrollado	paese in via di sviluppo paese meno sviluppato	Entwicklungsland unterentwickeltes Land
esperanza de vida expectativa de vida	vita media speranza di vita	Lebenserwartung
esperanza de vida al nacer vida media	vita media alla nascita speranza di vita alla nascita durata media di vita vita media dei neonati	Lebenserwartung bei der Geburt Lebenserwartung der Neugebor- enen durchschnittliche Lebensdauer
vida mediana vida probable	vita mediana vita mediana alla nascita vita probabile vita probabile dei neonati	mittlere Lebensdauer wahrscheinliche Lebensdauer
lapso de vida	longevità	Lebensspanne
tabla de mortalidad tabla de vida	tavola di mortalità	Sterbetafel
tabla abreviada de mortalidad	tavola abbreviata di mortalità tavola di mortalità abbreviata	abgekürzte Sterbetafel
tabla completa de mortalidad tabla de mortalidad detallada	tavola completa di mortalità tavola di mortalità completa	vollständige Sterbetafel
alfabeto, m.	alfabeta non analfabeta	des Lesens und Schreibens kun- dige Person
nivel de vida	tenore di vita standard di vita	höhe der Lebenshaltung Lebenshaltungsniveau Lebensstandard
longevidad duración de la vida	longevità durata della vita	normale Lebensdauer

English	French
male, n.	individu du sexe masculin
man	homme
marital status	situation matrimoniale
civil status	état matrimonial
conjugal status	
marriage	mariage
	union légitime
marriage, common-law. *See* union, consensual.	
marriage, duration of	durée du mariage
marriage rate	taux de nuptialité
married man	homme marié
married woman	femme mariée
mean, adj.	moyen, m.
average, adj.	
mean, n.	moyenne
average, n.	moyenne arithmétique
mean deviation	écart absolu moyen
mean length of life. *See* life expectancy at birth.	
median, adj.	médian, m.
median, n.	médiane
median length of life. *See* life, median length of.	
menarche	première règle
menopause	ménopause
climacteric	
menstrual cycle	cycle menstrual
menstruation	menstruation
migrant	migrant, m.
migration	migration
	mouvement migratoire
migration, forced	migration forcée

Spanish	Italian	German
individuo del sexo masculino	maschio	Person männlichen Geschlechts
varón	uomo	Mann
hombre		
estado civil	stato civile	Familienstand
estado matrimonial	stato matrimoniale	
situación matrimonial	stato coniugale	
matrimonio	matrimonio	(rechtmässige) Ehe
casamiento		(legale) Ehe
duración del matrimonio	durata del matrimonio	Ehedauer
tasa de nupcialidad	tasso di nuzialità	Heiratsrate
	misura della nuzialità	Heiratsziffer
	indice di nuzialità	Eheschliessungsziffer
hombre casado	uomo sposato	verheirateter Mann
mujer casada	donna sposata	verheiratete Frau
	donna coniugata	
medio, m.	medio, m.	durchschnittlich
media	media	Durchschnitt
media aritmética		Mittelwert
promedio		arithmetisches Mittel
desviación media	deviazione dalla media	(einfache) mittlere Abweichung
	scostamento semplice medio	
	scarto semplice medio	
mediano, m.	mediano, m.	zentral
mediana	mediana	Zentralwert
valor central		Median
primera menstruación	menarca (pubertà)	erste Monatsregel
primera regla		Menarche
menopausia	menopausa	Menopause
	climaterio	Klimakterium
ciclo menstrual	ciclo mestruale	Monatszyklus
	periodo mestruale	
menstruación	mestruazione	Menstruation
migrante	migrante	Wanderer, m.
migración	migrazione	Wanderung
migración forzosa	migrazione forzata	Zwangswanderung
	migrazione coatta	Vertreibung

25

English	French
migration, internal	migration interne migration intérieure
migration, international	migration internationale
migration, net	migration nette balance migratoire solde migratoire
migration, return remigration	migration de retour
minority	minorité
miscarriage. *See* abortion.	
mobility. *See* geographical mobility; social mobility.	
modal	modal, m.
mode	mode
model, n.	modèle
moral restraint. *See* preventive check.	
morbidity	morbidité
mortality	mortalité
mortality, differential	mortalité différentielle
mortality, fetal	mortalité fétale mortalité intra-utérine
mortality, infant	mortalité infantile
mortality, maternal puerperal mortality	mortalité liée à la maternité mortalité maternelle
mortality, neonatal	mortalité néonatale
mortality, perinatal	mortalité périnatale
mortality, post-neonatal	mortalité post(-néo)natale
mortality rate. *See* death rate.	

Spanish	Italian	German
migración interna	migrazione interna	Binnenwanderung
migración internacional	migrazione internazionale migrazione con l'estero migrazione estera	internationale Wanderung
migración neta saldo migratorio	migrazione netta saldo migratorio	Wanderungsbilanz Wanderungssaldo Nettowanderung
migración de retorno	rimpatrio migrazione di ritorno	Rückwanderung
minoría	minoranza	Minderheit
modal	modale	modal
moda modo valor dominante	moda valore più frequente norma	häufigster Wert dichtester Wert Modus
modelo	modello	Modell
morbilidad	morbilità morbosità	Erkrankungshäufigkeit Morbidität
mortalidad	mortalità	Sterblichkeit Mortalität
mortalidad diferencial	mortalità differenziale	differenzielle Sterblichkeit
mortalidad fetal	mortalità intrauterina mortalità prenatale mortalità fetale	intrauterine Sterblichkeit Fötalsterblichkeit
mortalidad infantil	mortalità infantile	Säuglingssterblichkeit
mortalidad maternal mortalidad puerperal	mortalità materna mortalità dovuta alla maternità mortalità puerperale	Müttersterblichkeit
mortalidad neonatal mortalidad precoz mortineonatalidad	mortalità neonatale	Frühsterblichkeit der Säuglinge Neonatalsterblichkeit
mortalidad perinatal	mortalità perinatale	perinatale Sterblichkeit geburtsnahe Sterblichkeit
mortalidad postneonatal	mortalidà post-neonatale	Spät-Säuglingssterblichkeit Post-Neonatalsterblichkeit Post-Natalsterblichkeit

English	French
mortality rate, cause-specific	taux de mortalité par cause(s)
mortality table. *See* life table.	
mother tongue native language	langue maternelle
natality. *See* fertility.	
nation	nation
national origin	nationalité d'origine
nationality	nationalité citoyenneté
native-born	né dans le pays, m.
native language. *See* mother tongue.	
natural area	aire naturelle région naturelle
natural increase	accroissement naturel
naturalization	naturalisation
negative growth. *See* population decline.	
net	net, m.
never married. *See* single.	
nomad	nomade
nonresponse	défaut de réponse non-réponse
not stated. *See* unknown.	
number, n. figure, n.	nombre (absolu)
number, round	nombre rond
nuptiality	nuptialité

Spanish	Italian	German
tasa específica de mortalidad por causa(s)	tasso di mortalità per causa quoziente di mortalità per causa	Sterbeziffer nach Todesursache(n)
lengua materna lengua nativa	lingua materna madre lingua	Muttersprache
nación	nazione	Nation Volk Staat
nacionalidad de origen	nazionalità d'origine	nationale Herkunft Staatsangehörigkeit bei der Geburt
nacionalidad	cittadinanza nazionalità	Staatsangehörigkeit Staatsbürgerschaft Nationalität
nacido en el país, m.	nato nel paese, m.	Inländer, m. Eingeborener, m. im Inland Geborener, m.
área natural	regione naturale	Naturraum
crecimiento natural crecimiento vegetativo crecimiento fisiológico	accrescimento naturale incremento naturale	natürlicher Bevölkerungszuwachs Geborenenüberschuss Geburtenüberschuss
naturalización	naturalizzazione acquisto della cittadinanza	Einbürgerung Naturalisierung Naturalisation
neto, m.	netto, m.	Netto-
nómada	nomade	Nomade
falta de respuesta sin respuesta no consta	mancata risposta nessuna risposta	Nichtbeantwortung
número (absoluto) cifra	numero cifra	Zahl Grundzahl
número redondeado	cifra rotonda cifra tonda	runde Zahl
nupcialidad	nuzialità	Heiratshäufigkeit

English	French
occupation	profession
offspring progeny	progéniture
old age	vieillesse
overpopulation	surpopulation surpeuplement
ovulation	ovulation
ovum	ovule
owner landlord	propriétaire
parenthood	paternité
parents	parents
parity birth order	parité rang de naissance rang d'accouchement
people (nation)	nation
percentage percent	pourcentage
periodic abstinence. *See* rhythm method.	
person. *See* individual.	
person of no fixed abode. *See* vagrant.	
pessary. *See* diaphragm.	
pill. *See* contraceptive pill.	
population	population peuplement
population, active	population active
population, agricultural farm population	population (active) agricole population vivant de l'agriculture
population, closed	population fermée
population decline negative growth	décroissement de la population accroissement négatif

Spanish	Italian	German
ocupación profesión	occupazione attività individuale professione	Beruf
hijos	discendenza prole figli figliolanza progenie	Nachkommen Nachwuchs Kinder
vejez	vecchiaia età senile	fortgeschrittenes Alter hohes Alter
sobrepoblación	sovrapopolazione sovrapopolamento	Übervölkerung Überbevölkerung
ovulación	ovulazione	Eiausstoss Ovulation
óvulo	uovo	Ei
propietario, m.	proprietario, m.	Eigentümer, m. Hauswirt, m.
paternidad	paternità, maternità	Elternschaft
padres	genitori	Eltern
paridez orden de nacimiento	parità ordine di nascita	Geburtenfolge Rangfolge Ordnungszahl der Geburt
pueblo nación	nazione	Volk
porcentaje por ciento	percentuale	Prozentzahl Prozentsatz
población	popolazione	Bevölkerung (statistische) Population
población activa	popolazione attiva	Erwerbspersonen
población agropecuaria población agrícola	popolazione agricola popolazione vivente di agricol- tura	landwirtschaftliche Bevölkerung Berufszugehörige der Landwirt- schaft
población cerrada	popolazione chiusa	geschlossene Bevölkerung
descenso de población crecimiento negativo	popolazione in declino declino della popolazione	Bevölkerungsrückgang Abnahme der Bevölkerung

English	French
population, de facto enumerated population	population présente population de fait population de facto
population, de jure resident population	population résidente population de résidence habituelle population de droit population de jure
population density	densité de la population intensité du peuplement
population, enumerated. *See* population, de facto.	
population forecast	perspective démographique prévision démographique perspective de population
population growth	accroissement de la population
population, mean	effectif moyen de la population population moyenne
population, open	population ouverte
population optimum optimum population	population optimale optimum de peuplement
population policy	politique démographique politique de population
population pressure	pression démographique
population projection	projection démographique projection de la population
population pyramid	pyramide des âges
population, quasi-stable	population quasistable
population register	registre de population fiche fichier de population
population, resident. *See* population, de jure.	
population, stable	population stable
population, standard	population type
population, stationary	population stationnaire

Spanish	Italian	German
	incremento negativo crescita negativa	Bevölkerungsschrumpfung negatives Wachstum
población presente población de hecho	popolazione presente popolazione di fatto popolazione enumerata popolazione censita	ortsanwesende Bevölkerung
población residente población de derecho	popolazione residente popolazione legale popolazione di diritto popolazione de jure	Wohnbevölkerung
densidad de población	intensità del popolamento densità della popolazione	Bevölkerungsdichte Besiedlungsdichte
pronóstico demográfico predicción demográfica perspectiva demográfica previsión demográfica	previsione demografica prospettiva demografica	Bevölkerungsvoraussage Bevölkerungsprognose
crecimiento de la población	crescita della popolazione incremento della popolazione	Bevölkerungswachstum Wachstum der Bevölkerung Bevölkerungszunahme Bevölkerungszuwachs
población media número medio de personas	popolazione media	mittlere Bevölkerung
población abierta	popolazione aperta	offene Bevölkerung
optimo de población población óptima	popolazione ottima optimum di popolazione	Bevölkerungsoptimum optimale Bevölkerung
política de la población	politica della popolazione politica demografica	Bevölkerungspolitik
presión de la población presión demográfica	pressione demografica	Bevölkerungsdruck
proyección de la población proyección demográfica	proiezione demografica	Bevölkerungsvorausberechnung Bevölkerungsprojektion
pirámide de edades	piramide delle età	Alterspyramide
población cuasi estable	popolazione quasi stabile	quasi-stabile Bevölkerung
registro de la población	registro della popolazione	Bevölkerungsregister
población estable	popolazione stabile	stabile Bevölkerung
población estandár	popolazione tipo	Standardbevölkerung
población estacionaria	popolazione stazionaria	stationäre Bevölkerung

English	French
population statistics	statistiques démographiques
positive check	obstacle répressif
pregnancy	grossesse
gestation	gestation
	gravidité
prematurity (of births)	prématurité
prevalence rate	proportion des malades
preventive check	obstacle préventif
moral restraint	contrainte morale
probability	probabilité
	quotient
probable length of life. *See* life, median length of.	
productivity	productivité
progeny. *See* offspring.	
proportion	proportion
provisional	provisoire
puberty	puberté
public health	santé publique
punch, n.	(machine) perforatrice
punch card	carte mécanographique
	carte perforée
questionnaire	questionnaire
race, n.	race
radix (of a life table)	racine
range	étendue
rate	taux

Spanish	Italian	German
estadísticas demográficas estadísticas de la población	statistiche demografiche	Bevölkerungsstatistiken
control positivo	ostacolo repressivo freno repressivo	repressive Hemmung
embarazo gestación preñez	gravidanza gestazione	Schwangerschaft
prematuridad	prematurità	Frühgeburt
tasa de prevalencia proporción de enfermos	proporzione di malati	Krankenbestandsziffer
control preventivo freno moral	ostacolo preventivo freno morale freno preventivo	präventive Hemmung moralische Enthaltung
probabilidad	probabilità	Wahrscheinlichkeit
productividad	produttività	Produktivität
proporción razón	proporzione	Gliederungszahl Anteil Quote
provisional	provvisorio, m. preliminario, m.	vorläufig provisorisch
pubertad	pubertà	Pubertät
salud pública sanidad pública salubridad pública	sanità pubblica	öffentliches Gesundheitswesen staatliches Gesundheitswesen
máquina perforadora	macchina perforatrice	Lochmaschine Locher
ficha perforada	scheda perforata scheda meccanografica	Lochkarte
cuestionario	questionario	Fragebogen
raza	razza	Rasse
raíz (de la tabla de mortalidad)	radice	Ausgangsmasse Radixbestand
campo de variación recorrido alcance amplitud	campo di variazione	Variationsbreite
tasa cociente	tasso quoziente	Häufigkeitsziffer Häufigkeitskoeffizient

ratio	rapport
refined figure	résultat élaboré
refugee	réfugié, m.
region. *See* area.	
registration	enrégistrement
relationship (to head of household)	lien
	relation
relatives	parents
kin	apparentés
religion	religion
	confession
remarriage	remariage
remigration. *See* migration, return.	
reproduction	procréation
reproduction rate, gross	taux brut de reproduction
reproduction rate, net	taux net de reproduction
residence. *See* dwelling unit.	
respondent (census)	recensé, m.
revised	révisé, m.

Spanish	Italian	German
	saggio coefficiente	Rate
razón proporción relación	rapporto	Verhältniszahl Beziehungszahl
cifra calculada	dato elaborato*	bearbeitetes Ergebniss abgeleitete Zahl
refugiado, m.	profugo, m. rifugiato, m.	Flüchtling Vertriebener, m. Heimatsvertriebener, m.
registro	registrazione	Registrierung
parentesco	relazione (col capofamiglia)	Stellung
parientes	parenti affini congiunti	Verwandte Blutsverwandte
religión	religione confessione religiosa	Religionsbekenntnis Glaubensbekenntnis
matrimonio sucesivo	secondo matrimonio (literally, second marriage) matrimonio successivo al primo	Wiederverheiratung
procreación	procreazione riproduttività	Zeugung Erzeugung Hervorbringung

tasa bruta de reproducción	tasso lordo di riproduttività fem-
	   inile
	saggio lordo di riproduttività
	   feminile
	saggio lordo di riproduttività
		Bruttoreproduktionsrate
		rohe Reproduktionsziffer

tasa neta de reproducción	tasso netto di riproduttività fem-
	   inile
	saggio netto di riproduttività
	   feminile
	saggio netto di riproduttività
		Nettoreproduktionsrate
		reine Reproduktionsziffer

respondente censado, m. inscrito, m.	censito, m. intervistato, m.	erfasste Person gezählte Person
revisado, m.	riveduto, m.	berichtigt

*Gives the sense of the English phrase but is seldom used.

English	French
corrected	rectifié, m.
	corrigé, m.
rhythm method	(méthode de) continence périodique
periodic abstinence	
risk	risque
chance	
rural	rural, m.
salpingectomy	tubectomie
sample, n.	échantillon
sample, probability	échantillon probabiliste
sample, representative	échantillon représentatif
sample survey	enquête par sondage
sampling, n.	sondage
sampling, area	sondage aréolaire
sampling, cluster	sondage en grappes
sampling error	erreur d'échantillonnage
sampling, stratified	sondage stratifié
scatter. *See* dispersion.	
schedule, n.	bulletin (of a survey)
	feuille (of a census)
segregation	ségrégation
self-enumeration	autorecensement
	autodénombrement
senility	sénilité

Spanish	Italian	German
corregido, m.	rettificato, m.	bereinigt
rectificado, m.	depurato, m.	verbessert
método del ritmo	ritmo	periodische Enthaltsamkeit
abstinencia periódica	metodo della continenza period-ica	Methode nach Ogino-Knaus
riesgo	rischio	Risiko
	caso	Aussicht
		Chance
rural	rurale	ländlich
salpingectomía	salpingectomia	Salpingektomie
muestra	campione	Stichprobe
muestra aleatoria	sondaggio probabilistico	Zufallsstichprobe
muestra al azar	campione probabilistico	
muestra representativa	campione rappresentativo	repräsentative Stichprobe
encuesta por muestreo	indagine campionario	Stichprobenerhebung
encuesta por sondeo	sondaggio campionario	
encuesta por muestra	inchiesta campionaria	
sobrevisión muestral	inchiesta por sondaggio	
muestreo	rilevazione campionaria	Stichprobenverfahren
sondeo	sondaggio	
encuesta		
muestra por áreas	sondaggio per aree	Flächenstichprobe
muestreo por conglomerados	campionamento a grappolo	Klumpenauswahl
muestreo por racimos	sondaggio a grappolo	
error de muestreo	errore di campionamento	Stichprobenfehler
muestra estratificada	campionamento stratificato	geschichtete Stichprobe
	sondaggio casuale stratificato	
planilla	scheda	Zählblatt
formulario	foglio	
boletín	elenco	
hoja	lista	
	programma	
segregación	segregazione	Bevölkerungstrennung
	isolamento	Segregation
autoenumeración	autoenumerazione	Selbstzählung
autoinscripción		Selbstausfüllung (eines Fragebo-gens)
senilidad	senilità	Altersschwäche
		Senilität

English	French
series	série
set, n.	ensemble
sex	sexe
sex-age-specific rate	taux par sexe et par groupe d'âges
sex ratio	rapport de masculinité
sexual intercourse. *See* coitus.	
sheath. *See* condom.	
siblings	fratrie
significance, level of	seuil de signification
	niveau de signification
simulation	simulation
single	célibataire (définitif)
never married	
SMA. *See* standard metropolitan area.	
smoothing (of a curve)	ajustement
	lissage
social class	classe sociale
social mobility	mobilité sociale
social stratification	stratification sociale
socio-economic group	groupe social
	groupe socio-économique
	catégorie sociale
sorter (machine)	(machine) trieuse
soul. *See* individual.	
spacing (of births), n.	échelonnement (des naissances)
	espacement (des naissances)
spatial distribution. *See* geographical distribution.	
sperm	spermatozoïde
spinster	célibataire du sexe féminin
sponge (contraceptive)	éponge vaginale

Spanish	Italian	German
serie	serie successione	Serie Aneinanderreihung
conjunto	insieme	Beobachtungsreihe
sexo	sesso	Geschlecht
tasa por sexo y por grupos de edades	tasso specifico per sesso ed età quoziente specifico per sesso ed età	alters- und geschlechtsspezi-fische Rate Ziffer nach dem Geschlecht und nach Altersgruppen
relación de masculinidad	rapporto di mascolinità rapporto dei sessi	Geschlechtsverhältnis Geschlechtsproportion Sexualproportion
fratria	fratellanza	Geschwister
nivel de significación	livello di significatività	Sicherheitsgrenze Signifikanzgrenze Signifikanzniveau
simulación	simulazione	Simulation
soltero, m célibe	celibe celibe e nubile	ledig
suavizamiento	perequazione graduazione	glätten (einer Kurve) Ausgleichung
clase social	classe sociale	soziale Schicht Gesellschaftsschicht
movilidad social	mobilità sociale circolazione sociale	soziale Mobilität
estratificación social	stratificazione sociale	soziale Schichtung
grupo socioeconómico grupo social categoría social	gruppo socio-economico categoria socio-economica	sozio-ökonomische Gruppe sozio-professionelle Gruppe
maquina clasificadora	classificatore macchina selezionatrice	Sortiermaschine
intervalo intergenesico	intervallo spazio	Geburtenabstand
espermatozoide	spermatozoo	Spermatozoon
soltera	nubile	Junggesellin
esponja vaginal	spugna vaginale	Scheidenschwämmchen

English	French
spouse	époux, m.; épouse, f.
	conjoint, m.; conjointe, f.
squatter	occupant sans titre
standard deviation	écart-type
standard error	erreur-type
standard metropolitan area	agglomération (multicommunale)
agglomeration	conurbation
conurbation	agglomération urbaine
standard of living. *See* living, level of.	
standardization, direct method of	méthode de la population type
standardization, indirect method of	méthode des taux types
standardized (of a rate)	comparatif, m.
state, n.	état
sterility	stérilité
infecundity	infertilité
sterilization	stérilisation
stillbirth	mortinatalité
	mortinaissance
subject, n.	sujet
subpopulation	sous-population
subsample	sous-échantillon

Spanish	Italian	German
cónyuge esposo, m.; esposa, f.	sposo, m.; sposa, f. coniuge	Ehegatte, m.; Ehegattin, f.
ocupante sin título	occupante senza titolo	Okkupant, m. Ansiedler auf fremden Boden, m.
desviación estandar(d)	scostamento quadratico medio squarto quadratico medio	mittlere (quadratische) Abweichung Standardabweichung durchschnittliche quadratische Abweichung
error típico error "estandard" error standard	errore quadratico medio errore medio	mittlere Abweichung Standardfehler
áre metropolitana aglomeración multimunicipal agrupación urbana	agglomerazione (multicomunale) metropolitana agglomerato (multicomunale) area metropolitana conurbazione	(vielgemeindliche) Agglomeration städtische Agglomeration Konurbation
método directo de estandar(d)ización	standardizzazione diretta normalizzazione diretta metodo della popolazione tipo	direkte Standardisierungsmethode
método indirecto de estandar(d)ización	standardizzazione indiretta normalizzazione indiretta metodo della mortalità tipo metodo dei coefficienti tipo metodo della correzione indiretta	indirekte Standardisierungsmethode
comparativa, f. estandar(d)izada, f.	standardizato, m. normalizzato, m. comparativo, m.	standardisiert
estado	stato	Staat
esterilidad	sterilità infertilità	Unfruchtbarkeit Sterilität
esterilización	sterilizzazione	Sterilisation Sterilisierung Unfruchtbarmachung
mortinatalidad nacido muerto, m.	natimortalità	Totgeburt
sujeto, m.	suddito, m. soggetto, m.	Staatsbürger, m.
subpoblación	sottopopolazione frazione della popolazione subpopolazione	Teilbevölkerung Bevölkerungsgruppe
submuestra	sottocampione subcampione	Unterstichprobe

43

English	French
subsistence level	minimum physiologique
suburb	banlieue
survey, n.	enquête
survival, probability of	probabilité de survie
survivor	survivant, m.
table, n.	table
tabulate	mettre en tableaux
tabulation, cross-	tableau à multiple entrée
tenant	locataire
territory. *See* area.	
time series	série chronologique
total years lived	nombre des années vécues
town. *See* city.	
transient, n.	personne de passage
trend	mouvement général
	tendance générale
true rate. *See* intrinsic rate.	
tubal ligation	stérilisation tubaire
underdeveloped country. *See* less developed country.	
underenumeration	lacune d'énumération
underpopulation	sous-population
	sous-peuplement
underregistration	lacune d'enrégistrement

Spanish	Italian	German
nivel de subsistencia mínimo vital	limite di sussistenza livello di sussistenza	(physiologisches) Existenzmini- mum
suburbio	suburbio sobborgo	Vorort
encuesta	inchiesta indagine	Befragung Rundfrage
probabilidad de sobrevivencia probabilidad de supervivencia	probabilità di sopravvivenza probabilità di vita	Überlebenswahrscheinlichkeit
sobreviviente superviviente	sopravvivente	Überlebender, m
tabla cuadro	tavola	Tabelle Tafel
tabular	tabulare	tabellieren
tabulación cruzada tabulación de múltiple entrada	tavola con entrate multiple tabella a plurima entrata tabella a multiple entrata	Kombinationstabelle
inquilino, m. arrendatario, m.	inquilino, m. locatario, m.	Mieter, m.
serie cronológica serie de tiempo	serie storica serie temporale serie cronologica	Zeitreihe
total de años vividos	numero totale di anni vissuti	durchlebte Zeit Gesamtzahl der durchlebten Jahre
transeúnte	persona temporaneamente pre- sente persona di passaggio	Durchreisender, m.
tendencia	tendenza (generale) variazione secolare tendenza di fondo	Hauptrichtung Grundrichtung Trend
ligación de tubos	legamento delle tube	Tubenligatur
subenumeración	sottoenumerazione	Untererfassung
subpoblación	sottopopolazione sottopopolamento	Untervölkerung Unterbevölkerung
subregistro	sottoregistrazione lacuna nella registrazione	lückenhafte Registrierung

English	French
unemployed, adj.	sans emploi
unemployed, n.	chômeur, m.
union	union
union, consensual	union libre union consensuelle mariage coutumier
union, free concubinage	union illégitime mariage consensuel
unknown not stated	non-déclaré, m. indéterminé, m. non-spécifié, m. mal défini, m. mal désigné, m.
unmarried person. *See* bachelor; single; spinster.	
urban	urbain, m.
urbanization	urbanisation
uterus womb	utérus
vagrant person of no fixed abode	personne sans résidence fixe personne sans domicile
variable, n.	variable
variation variability	variabilité
vasectomy	vasectomie
viable (of a fetus)	viable
village	village
vital revolution. *See* demographic transition.	
vital statistics	statistique de l'état civil
weight (statistical)	poid

46

Spanish	Italian	German
desempleado, m. sin empleo	disoccupato, m.	erwerbslos arbeitslos
desempleado, m.	disoccupato, m.	Erwerbsloser, m. Arbeitsloser, m. Beschäftigungsloser, m.
unión	unione	Verbindung
unión consensual unión libre	unione consensuale	Konkubinat
unión ilegítima concubinato	unione libera concubinato	freie Ehe eheähnliche Gemeinschaft
desconocido, m. mal definido, m. mal especificado, m. sin información	sconosciuto, m. non indicato, m. mal definito, m. non specificato, m. ignoto, m.	ohne Angabe unbekannt nicht bezeichnet nicht angegeben
urbano, m.	urbano, m.	städtisch
urbanización	urbanizzazione urbanesimo	Verstädterung
útero	utero	Uterus Gebärmutter
vagabundo, m. persona sin residencia fija persona sin domicilio	persona senza fissa dimora	Nichtsesshafter, m. Obdachloser, m. Person ohne festen Wohnort Vagabund, m.
variable	variabile	Variable Veränderliche
variación variabilidad	variabilità variazione	Streuung Dispersion
vasectomía	vasectomia	Sterilisation (des Mannes)
viable	vitale	lebensfähig
aldea lugar villa localidad	paese villaggio borgo borgata	Dorf
estadísticas vitales	statistiche dello stato civile	Statistik der natürlichen Bevölkerungsbewegung
coeficiente de ponderación	coefficiente di ponderazione peso	Wägungsfaktor Gewicht

weighted mean	moyenne ponderée
weighted average	
withdrawal. *See* coitus interruptus.	
woman. *See* female, n.	
womb. *See* uterus.	
younging (of a population)	rajeunissement (démographique)

Spanish	Italian	German
media ponderada	media ponderata	gewogenes arithmetisches Mittel
promedio ponderado		gewogener Durchschnitt
rejuvenecimiento		Verjüngung
(población) rejuveneciéndose		
con estructura de edades mas		
jovenes		

English–Japanese and Chinese
(Pin-yin and Wade-Giles)

English	Japanese	Japanese Transliteration
abortion	流産	ryūzan
	堕胎	datai
	中絶	chūzetsu
abortion, induced	人工妊娠中絶	jinkō ninshin chūzetsu
abortion, spontaneous	自然流産	shizen ryūzan
miscarriage	流産	ryūzan
acculturation	文化変容	bunka henyō
accuracy	正確さ	seikakusa
adolescence	青年期	seinenki
adolescent, n.	青年	seinen
adult, n.	成人	seijin
	大人	otona
age	年齢	nenrei
age distribution	年齢分布	nenrei bunpu
age structure	年齢構造	nenrei kōzō
age group(ing)	年齢階級	nenrei-gun
age bracket	年齢層	nenreisō
age-specific rate	年齢別特殊率	nenrei-betsu tokushu-ritsu

agglomeration. *See* standard metropolitan area.

English	Japanese	Japanese Transliteration
aging, n.	老齢化	rōreika
	老年化	rōnenka
	老化	rōka
	高齢化	kōreika
alien, n.	外国人	gaikokujin
analysis	分析	bunseki
area	地域	chiiki
territory	領土	ryōdo
region	領域	ryōiki
	地域	chiiki
arrival (of immigrants)	入国(移民の)	nyūkoku (imin no)
assimilation	同化	dōka

attribute. *See* characteristic.

average. *See* mean, adj.; mean, n.

baby. *See* infant.

English	Japanese	Japanese Transliteration
bachelor	独身(者)	dokushin (sha)
base, n.	基準	kijun
birth	出生	shusshō (or shussei)
	出産	shussan

Chinese	Pin-yin	Wade-Giles
墮胎	duo tai	to t'ai
人工墮胎	ren gong duo tai	jen-kung to t'ai
自然墮胎	zi ran duo tai	tzu-jan to t'ai
涵化	han hua	han-hua
準確	zhun que	chun-ch'üeh
青年期	qing nian qi	ch'ing-nien ch'i
青少年	qing shao nian	ch'ing shao nien
成人	cheng ren	ch'eng-jen
年齡	nian ling	nien-ling
年齡分佈	nian ling fen bu	nien-ling fen-pu
年齡結構	nian ling jie gou	nien-ling chieh-kou
年齡組	nian ling zu	nien-ling tsu
年齡叢	nian ling cong*	nien-ling ts'ung*
年別率	nian bie lü	nien-pieh lü
老化	lao hua	lao-hua
外國人	wai guo ren	wai-kuo jen
分析	fen xi	fen-hsi
地區	di qu	ti-ch'ü
地域	di yu	ti-yü
區域	qu yu	ch'ü-yü
到達	dao da	tao-ta
同化	tong hua	t'ung-hua
獨身	du shen	tu-shen
基準	ji zhun	chi-chun
生育	sheng yu	sheng-yü

*Translates the English but is not generally used.

English	Japanese	Japanese Transliteration
birth control	産児制限 出生調節	sanji seigen shusshō chōsetsu
birth interval	出生間隔	shusshō kankaku
birth, live	出生 生産	shusshō seizan
birth, multiple	複産	fukusan
birth order. *See* parity.		
birth, premature	早産	sōzan
birth rate	出生率	shusshō-ritsu
block, n.	ブロック	burroku
boarder 　　lodger	下宿人 間借人	geshukunin magarinin
bunching. *See* heaping.		
capital (city)	首都	shuto
celibacy	独身生活 禁欲生活	dokushin seikatsu kinyoku seikatsu
census	国勢調査 センサス	kokusei chōsa sensasu
census tract	国勢調査区 センサス・トラクト	kokusei chōsa ku sensasu torakuto
central city	中心都市	chūshin toshi
cervical cap. *See* diaphragm.		
chance. *See* risk.		
characteristic 　　attribute	標識 属性	hyōshiki zokusei
child-woman ratio	婦人子供比率	fujin kodomo hiritsu
citizen	市民	shimin
city 　　town	市 都市 町	shi toshi machi
civil status. *See* marital status.		
classify	分類する	bunruisuru
climacteric. *See* menopause.		
code, v.	符号化する	fugōkasuru
cohabitation. *See* coitus.		
cohort	同時出生集団 コーホート	dōji shusshō shūdan kōhōto

Chinese	Pin-yin	Wade-Giles
生育節制	sheng yu jie zhi	sheng-yü chieh-chih
生育間隔	sheng yu jian ge	sheng-yü chien-ko
活生育	huo sheng yu	huo-sheng yü
多生育	duo sheng yu	to-sheng yü
早產	zao chan	tsao-ch'an
出生率	chu sheng lü	ch'u-sheng lü
地段	di duan	ti-tuan
寄居者	ji ju zhe	chi-chü-chê
首都	shou du	shou-tu
獨身生活	du shen sheng huo	tu-shen sheng-huo
普查	pu cha	p'u-ch'a
普查區	pu cha qu	p'u-ch'a ch'ü
中心都市	zhong xin du shi	chung hsin tu shih
特徵	te zheng	t'e-cheng
孩婦比	hai fu bi	hai fu pi
公民	gong min	kung-min
城市	cheng shi	ch'eng-shih
鎮	zhen	chen
分類	fen lei	fen-lei
法則	fa ze	fa-tsê
一羣	yi qun	yi-ch'ün
同隊	tong dui	t'ung-tui

55

English	Japanese	Japanese Transliteration
cohort fertility. *See* fertility.		
cohort, synthetic	合成コーホート	gōsei kōhōto
coitus 　sexual intercourse 　cohabitation	性交	seikō
coitus interruptus 　withdrawal	性交中絶法 抜去法	seikō chūzetsuhō bakkyohō
color (of skin)	色(皮膚の)	iro (hifu no)
commuter	通勤人口	tsūkin jinkō
commuting	通勤移動	tsūkin idō
computer (electronic)	電子計算機 コンピューター	denshi keisanki konpyūtā
conception	受胎 着床 妊娠	jutai chakushō ninshin
concubinage. *See* union.		
condom 　sheath	コンドーム	kondōmu
conjugal status. *See* marital status.		
contraception	避妊	hinin
contraceptive, n.	避妊器具	hinin kigu
contraceptive method	避妊法	hininhō
contraceptive, oral	ピル 経口避妊薬	piru keikō hinin yaku
contraceptive pill	避妊用ピル	hininyō piru
contraceptive, postcoital 　morning-after pill	性交後服用ピル モーニング・アフター・ピル	seikōgo fukuyō piru mōningu āfutā piru
conurbation. *See* standard metropolitan area.		
corrected. *See* revised.		
count, n.	集計	shūkei
country	国	kuni
couple (married)	夫婦	fūfu
cross-tabulation. *See* tabulation, cross.		
crude (of a rate)	普通(率)	futsū (ritsu)
data	資料 データ	shiryō dēta

Chinese	Pin-yin	Wade-Giles
塑造一羣	su zao yi qun*	su-tsao yi-ch'ün*
性交	xing jiao	hsing-chiao
同居	tong ju	t'ung-chü
性交中止	xing jiao zhong zhi	hsing-chiao chung-chih
膚色	fu se	fu-sê
通勤者	tong qin zhe*	t'ung-chin-chê*
通勤	tong qin*	t'ung-chin*
電腦	dian nao	tien-nao
懷孕	huai yun	huai-yün
保險套	bao xian tao	pao-hsien t'ao
避孕	bi yun	pi-yün
避孕藥物	bi yun yao wu	pi-yün yao-wu
避孕工具	bi yun gong ju	pi-yün kung-chü
避孕法	bi yun fa	pi-yün fa
口服避孕藥	kou fu bi yun yao	k'ou-fu pi-yün yao
避孕丸藥	bi yun wan yao	pi-yün wan-yao
性交後避孕丸	xing jiao hou bi yun wan	hsing-chiao hou pi-yün wan
晨後丸	chen hou wan	ch'en hou wan
數目	shu mu	shu-mu
國家	guo jia	kuo-chia
夫婦	fu fu	fu-fu
粗率	cu (lüi)	ts'u (lüi)
資料	zi liao	tzu-liao

*Translates the English but is not generally used.

English	Japanese	Japanese Transliteration
data, basic	基礎資料	kiso shiryō
crude data	粗資料	so-shiryō
primary data	原資料	gen shiryō
raw data	生の資料	nama no shiryō
death	死亡	shibō
death, cause of	死因	shiin
death certificate	死亡証明書	shibō shōmeisho
death, probability of	死亡確率	shibō kakuritsu
death rate	死亡率	shibō-ritsu
demographer	人口学者	jinkō gakusha
demographic transition	人口転換	jinkō tenkan
demographic revolution	人口革命	jinkō kakumei
vital revolution		
demography	人口学	jinkōgaku
denomination (religious)	デノミネーション	denominēshon
	宗派	shūha
departure (of emigrants)	出国(移民の)	shukkoku (imin no)
dependency ratio	従属指数	jūzoku shisū
dependent, n.	扶養者	fuyōsha
dependent children	扶養児童	fuyō jidō
depopulation	人口減少	jinkō genshō
diagram	図表	zuhyō
graph	グラフ	gurafu
diaphragm	隔膜(ペッサリー)	kakumaku (pessarī)
cervical cap	子宮頸管帽	shikyū keikanbō
pessary	ペッサリー	pessarī
difference	差異	sai
disability	無能力	munōryoku
disease	疾病	shippei
	病気	byōki
dispersion	分散(度)	bunsan (do)
scatter, n.	散布度	sanpudo
	ちらばり	chirabari
displaced person	難民	nanmin
distribution (frequency)	分布(度数)	bunpu (dosū)
divorce	離婚	rikon
dwelling unit	住居	jūkyo
residence		
ecology, human	人間生態学	ningen seitaigaku

Chinese	Pin-yin	Wade-Giles
基本資料	ji ben zi liao	chi-pen tzu-liao
粗資料	cu zi liao	ts'u tzu liao
原始資料	yuan shi zi liao	yüan-shih tzu-liao
生資料	sheng zi liao	sheng tzu-liao
死亡	si wang	szu-wang
死亡原因	si wang yuan yin	szu-wang yüan-yin
死亡證明	si wang zheng ming	szu-wang cheng-ming
死亡可能率	si wang ke neng lü	szu-wang k'o-neng lü
死亡率	si wang lü	szu-wang lü
人口統計學者	ren kou tong ji xue zhe	jen-k'ou t'ung-chi hsüeh-chê
人口變更	ren kou bian geng	jen-k'ou pien-keng
人口革命	ren kou ge ming	jen-k'ou ke-ming
人口統計學	ren kou tong ji xue	jen-k'ou t'ung-chi hsüeh
教派	jiao pai	chiao-p'ai
移出	yi chu	i-ch'u
依賴比	yi lai bi	yi-lai pi
眷屬	juan shu	chüan-shu
子女	juan shu zi nü	chüan-shu tzu-nü
人口減低	ren kou jian di	jen-k'ou chien-ti
圖表	tu biao	t'u-piao
子宮帽	zi gong mao	tzu-kung mao
差異	cha yi	ch'a-i
殘廢	can fei	ts'an-fei
疾病	ji bing	chi-ping
散佈	san bu	san-pu
移置人	yi zhi ren	i-chih jen
分布	fen bu	fen-pu
離婚	li hun	li-hun
住宅	zhu zhai	chu-chai
人文生態	ren wen sheng tai	jen-wen shang-t'ai

English	Japanese	Japanese Transliteration
economic development	経済発展	keizai hatten
economic growth	経済成長	keizai seichō

economic sector. *See* industry.

education, higher	高等教育	kōtō kyōiku
education, primary	初等教育	shotō kyōiku
education, secondary	中等教育	chūtō kyōiku
emigration	出国移民	shukkoku imin
employed	雇用者	koyōsha
endogenous (of a death)	内因性の(死因)	naiinsei no (shiin)
enumeration	実査	jissa
enumerator	調査者	chōsasha
	調査員	chōsain
epidemic, n.	伝染病	densenbyō
estimate, n.	推定値	suiteichi
estimation	推定	suitei
estimate, v.	推定する	suiteisuru
ethnic group	民族集団	minzoku shūdan
eugenics	優生学	yūseigaku
ever married, adj.	既婚の	kikon no
exogenous (of a death)	外因性の(死因)	gaiinsei no (shiin)

expectation of life. *See* life expectancy.

extrapolation	挿	gaisōhō
	補外法	hogaihō
family	家族	kazoku
family allowance	家族手当	kazoku teate
family subsidy		
family, nuclear	核家族	kaku kazoku
family planning	家族計画	kazoku keikaku
family size	家族規模	kazoku kibo

farm population. *See* population, agricultural.

fecundability	妊娠能力	ninshin nōryoku
	妊娠可能性	ninshin kanōsei
fecundity	妊娠力	ninshin ryoku
female, n.	女	on'na
woman	婦人	fujin
fertility	出生力	shusshō-ryoku
natality	出産力	shussan-ryoku
	出産能力	shussan nōryoku

60

Chinese	Pin-yin	Wade-Giles
經濟發展	jing ji fa zhan	ching-chi fa-chan
經濟成長	jing ji cheng zhang	ching-chi ch'eng-chang
高等教育	gao deng jiao yu	kao-teng chiao-yü
小學教育	xiao xue jiao yu	hsiao-hsüeh chiao-yü
中學教育	zhong xue jiao yu	chung-hsüeh chiao-yü
外移	wai yi	wai-i
就業	jiu ye	chiu-yeh
內發的	nei fa di	nei-fa-ti
查計	cha ji	ch'a-chi
查計員	cha ji yuan	ch'a-chi yüan
流行病	liu xing bing	liu-hsing ping
估計	gu ji	ku-chi
估計	gu ji	ku-chi
民族	min zu	min-tsu
優生學	you sheng xue	yu-sheng hsüeh
結過婚	jie guo hun	chieh-kuo hun
外因的	wai yin di	wai-yin-ti
外延法	wai yan fa	wai yen fa
家庭	jia ting	chia-t'ing
家庭津貼	jia ting jing tie	chia-t'ing chin-t'ieh
家庭補助	jia ting bu zhu	chia-t'ing pu-chu
核心家庭	he xin jia ting	ho-hsin chia-t'ing
家庭計劃	jia ting ji hua	chia-t'ing chi-hua
家庭大小	jia ting da xiao	chia-t'ing ta-hsiao
生殖力	sheng zhi li	sheng-chih li
	sheng zhi li	sheng-chih li
婦女	fu nü	fu-nü
生育力	sheng yu li	sheng-yü li

English	Japanese	Japanese Transliteration
fertility, cohort	コーホート出産力	kōhōto shussan-ryoku
	コーホート出生力	kōhōto shusshō-ryoku
fertility, completed	完結出生力	kanketsu shusshō-ryoku
fertility rate	総出生率	shusshō-ritsu
fertility rate, total	合計特殊出生率	gōkei tokushu shusshō-ritsu
	粗再生産率	so-saiseisan-ritsu
fertilization	受精	jusei
fetus	胎児	taiji
figure. *See* number.		
fluctuation	変動	hendō
follow-up, n.	フォロー・アップ	forō-appu
	追跡調査	tsuiseki chōsa
foreign-born	外国生まれ	gaikoku umare
form, n.	調査票	chōsahyō
generation	世代	sedai
generation, length of a	世代間隔	sedai kankaku
genetics	遺伝学	idengaku
geographical distribution	地理的分布	chiriteki bunpu
spatial distribution	空間的分布	kūkanteki bunpu
geographical mobility	地理的移動	chiriteki idō
spatial mobility	空間的移動	kūkanteki idō
geometric mean	幾何平均	kika heikin
geriatrics	老人病学	rōjinbyōgaku
gerontology	老年学	rōnengaku
gestation. *See* pregnancy.		
graph. *See* diagram.		
gross	総	sō
group	集団	shūdan
	群	gun
	グループ	gurūpu
hamlet	小村落	shō-sonraku
head. *See* household.		
heaping	集積	shūseki
bunching		
heredity	遺伝	iden
household	世帯	setai
household, head of a	世帯主	setai-nushi

Chinese	Pin-yin	Wade-Giles
同齡生育力	tong dui sheng yu li	t'ung-tui sheng-yü li
完全生育力	wan quan sheng yu li	wan-ch'üan sheng-yü li
生育率	sheng yu lü	sheng-yü lü
總生育率	zong sheng yu lü	tsung sheng-yü lü
受胎	shou tai	shou-t'ai
胚胎	pei tai	p'ei-t'ai
波動	bo dong	po-tung
追蹤	zhui zong	chui-tsung
國外生	gou wai sheng	kuo-wai sheng
表式	biao shi	piao-shi
世代	shi dai	shih-tai
世代長度	shi dai chang du	shih-tai ch'ang-tu
遺傳學	yi chuan xue	i-ch'uan hsüeh
地理分佈	di li fen bu	ti-li fen-pu
地理移動	di li yi dong	ti-li i-tung
幾何平均數	ji he ping jun shu	chi-ho p'ing-chün shu
老年病學	lao nian bing xue	lao-nien ping-hsüeh
老年學	lao nian xue	lao-nien hsüeh
總	zong	tsung
團體	tuan ti	t'uan-t'i
小村	xiao cun	hsiao-ts'un
羣集	qun ji	ch'ün-chi
堆積	dui ji	tui-chi
遺傳	yi chuan	i-ch'uan
戶口	hu kou	hu-k'ou
戶長	hu zhang	hu-chang
戶主	hu zhu	hu-chu

English	Japanese	Japanese Transliteration
household, member of a	世帯員 世帯人員	setaiin setai-jin'in
illegitimacy	庶出 非嫡出	shoshutsu hichakushutsu
illegitimate	庶出の 非嫡出の	shoshutsu no hichakushutsu no
immigration	移入民	inyūmin
incidence rate	罹患率	rikan-ritsu
index	指数	shisū
indicator	指標	shihyō
individual 　　person 　　soul	個人 人 人物	kojin hito jinbutsu
industry 　　sector of the economy	産業	sangyō
infant 　　baby	乳児 赤ん坊	nyūji akanbō
infecundity. *See* sterility.		
inhabitant	居住者	kyojūsha
interpolation	補間法	hokanhō
interviewer	面接者	mensetsusha
intra-uterine device 　　IUD	子宮内避妊器具 子宮内避妊装置	shikyūnai hinin kigu shikyūnai hinin sōchi
intrinsic rate 　　true rate	真正率	shinsei-ritsu
IUD. *See* intra-uterine device.		
kin. *See* relatives.		
lactation (prolonged)	授乳期間(延長した)	junyū kikan (enchō-shita)
landlord. *See* owner.		
language, native. *See* mother tongue.		
legitimacy	嫡出	chakushutsu
legitimate	嫡出の	chakushutsu no
length of life. *See* longevity.		
less developed country 　　underdeveloped country	低開発国	teikaihatsu koku
life expectancy 　　expectation of life	平均余命	heikin yomei

Chinese	Pin-yin	Wade-Giles
户員	hu yuan	hu-yüan
私生	si sheng	szu-sheng
私生的	si sheng di	szu-sheng-ti
移入	yi ru	i-ju
發病率	fa bing lü	fa-ping lü
指數	zhi shu	chih-shu
指標	zhi biao	chih-piao
個人	ge ren	ko-jen
人	ren	jen
工業	gong ye	kung-yeh
經濟部門	jing ji bu men	ching-chi pu-men
嬰孩	ying hai	ying-hai
居民	ju min	chü-min
內插法	nei cha fa	nei-ch'a fa
訪問員	fang wen yuan	fang-wen yüan
子宮內避孕器	zi gong nei bi yun qi	tzu-kung nei pi-yü-ch'i
固有率	gu you lü	ku yu lü
哺乳期(延長)	bu ru qi (yan chang)	pu-ju-ch'i (yen-ch'ang)
合法	he fa	ho-fa
合法的	he fa di	ho-fa-ti
次開發國家	ci kai fa guo jia	tz'u k'ai-fa kuo-chia
生命預期值	sheng ming yu qi zhi	sheng-ming yü-ch'i-chih

65

English	Japanese	Japanese Transliteration
life expectancy at birth mean length of life	平均寿命	heikin jumyō
life, median length of probable length of life	中央生存率	chūō seizon-ritsu
life span	寿命	jumyō
life table mortality table	生命表	seimeihyō
life table, abridged	簡速生命表 簡速静止人口表	kansoku seimeihyō kansoku seishi jinkōhyō
life table, complete	完全生命表	kanzen seimeihyō
literate person	読み書きできる人	yomikakidekiru hito
living, level of standard of living	生活水準	seikatsu suijun
lodger. See boarder.		
longevity length of life	寿命 長寿 生存期間	jumyō chōju seizon kikan
male, n. man	男	otoko

marital status
  civil status
  conjugal status
	配偶関係	haigū kankei

marriage	結婚 婚姻	kekkon kon'in
marriage, common-law. See union, consensual.		
marriage, duration of	婚姻期間 結婚持続期間	kon'in kikan kekkon jizoku kikan
marriage rate	婚姻率	kon'in-ritsu
married man	既婚男子	kikon danshi
married woman	既婚女子	kikon joshi
mean, adj. average	平均の	heikin no
mean, n. average	平均値	heikinchi
mean deviation	平均偏差	heikin hensa
mean length of life. See life expectancy at birth.		
median, adj.	中央の	chūōno
median, n.	メディアン 中央値	median chūōchi

Chinese	Pin-yin	Wade-Giles
初生生命預期值	chu sheng sheng ming yu qi zhi	ch'u-sheng sheng-ming yü-ch'i-chih
生命平均度	sheng ming ping jun du	sheng-ming p'ing-chün-tu
生命中位度	sheng ming zhong wei du	sheng-ming chung-wei tu
生命可能長度	sheng ming ke neng chang du	sheng-ming k'o-neng ch'ang-tu
生命幅度	sheng ming fu du	sheng-ming fu-tu
生命表	sheng ming biao	sheng-ming piao
簡要生命表	jian yao sheng ming biao	chien-yao sheng-ming piao
完整生命表	wan zheng sheng ming biao	wan-cheng sheng-ming piao
識字者	shi zi zhe	shih-tzu-chê
生活水平	sheng huo shui ping	sheng-huo shui-p'ing
生活程度	sheng huo cheng du	sheng-huo ch'eng-tu
壽命	shou ming	shou-ming
男	nan	nan
婚姻狀況	hun yin zhuang kuang	hun-yin chuang-k'uang
結婚	jie hun	chieh-hun
結婚久度	jie hun jiu du	chieh-hun chiu-tu
結婚率	jie hun lü	chieh-hun lü
已婚男人	yi hun nan ren	i-hun nan-jen
已婚婦女	yi hun fu nü	i-hun fu-nü
平均的	ping jun di	p'ing-chün-ti
平均數	ping jun shu	p'ing-chün shu
平均的差數	ping jun di cha shu	p'ing-chün-ti ch'a-shu
中位的	zhong wei di	chung-wei-ti
中位數	zhong wei shu	chung-wei shu

English	Japanese	Japanese Transliteration
median length of life. *See* life, median length of.		
menarche	初潮	shochō
menopause climacteric	月経閉止期間	gekkei heishi kikan
menstrual cycle	月経周期	gekkei shūki
menstruation	月経	gekkei
migrant	移住者	ijūsha
migration	人口移動 移住 移民	jinkō idō ijū imin
migration, forced	強制移住	kyōsei ijū
migration, internal	国内人口移動	kokunai jinkō idō
migration, international	国際移住 国際移動	kokusai ijū kokusai idō
migration, net	純人口移動	jun-jinkō idō
migration, return remigration	帰還移動	kikan idō
minority	少数民族 マイノリティ	shosū minzoku mainoritii
miscarriage. *See* abortion.		
mobility. *See* geographical mobility; social mobility.		
modal	モードの 最頻値の	mōdo no saihinchi no
mode	モード 最頻値	mōdo saihinchi
model, n.	模型 モデル	mokei moderu
moral restraint. *See* preventive check.		
morbidity	羅病率	ribyō-ritsu
mortality	死亡率 死亡力	shibō-ritsu shibō-ryoku
mortality, differential	差別死亡率	sabetsu shibō ritsu
mortality, fetal	胎児死亡率	taiji shibō ritsu
mortality, infant	乳児死亡率	nyūji shibō ritsu
mortality, maternal puerperal mortality	妊産婦死亡率	ninsanpu shibō ritsu
mortality, neonatal	新生児死亡率	shinseiji shibō ritsu
mortality, perinatal	周産期死亡率	shūsanki shibō ritsu

Chinese	Pin-yin	Wade-Giles
初潮	chu chao	ch'u-ch'ao
停經	ting jing	t'ing ching
經期	jing qi	ching-ch'i
月經	yue jing	yüeh-ching
移民	yi min	i-min
遷移	qian yi	ch'ien-i
強迫遷移	qiang po qian yi	ch'iang-p'o ch'ien-i
國內遷移	guo nei qian yi	kuo-nei ch'ien-i
國際遷移	guo ji qian yi	kuo-chi ch'ien-i
淨遷移	jing qian yi	ching ch'ien-i
回歸遷移	hui gui qian yi	hui-kui ch'ien-i
少數民族	shao shu min zu	shao-shu min-tsu
多數的	duo shu de	to-shu-te
方式	fang shi	fang-shih
典型	dian xing	tien-hsing
模型	mo xing	mo-hsing
疾病	ji bing	chi-ping
死亡	si wang	szu-wang
差別死亡	cha bie si wang	ch'a-pieh szu-wang
胎兒死亡	tai er si wang	t'ai-erh szu-wang
嬰兒死亡	yin er si wang	ying-erh szu-wang
產婦	chan fu si wang	ch'an-fu szu-wang
新生兒死亡	xin sheng er si wang	hsin-sheng-erh szu-wang
圍產死亡	wei chan si wang	wei-ch'an szu-wang

English	Japanese	Japanese Transliteration
mortality, post-neonatal	後期新生児死亡率	kōki shinseiji shibō ritsu
mortality rate. *See* death rate.		
mortality rate, cause-specific	死因別死亡率	shiinbetsu shibō ritsu
mortality table. *See* life table.		
mother tongue 　　native language	母国語	bokokugo
natality. *See* fertility		
nation	民族 国家	minzoku kokka
national origin	出身国	shusshin koku
nationality	国籍	kokuseki
native-born	本国生まれ	hongoku umare
native language. *See* mother tongue.		
natural area	自然地域	shizen chiiki
natural increase	自然増加	shizen zōka
naturalization	帰化	kika
negative growth. *See* population decline.		
net	純	jun
never married. *See* single.		
nomad	遊牧民	yūbokumin
nonresponse	無回答	mukaitō
not stated. *See* unknown.		
number, n. 　　figure, n.	数 数字	kazu sūji
number, round	概数	gaisū
nuptiality	結婚 婚姻	kekkon kon'in
occupation	職業	shokugyō
offspring 　　progeny	子供 子孫	kodomo shison
old age	老齢 老年	rōrei rōnen
overpopulation	過剰人口	kajō jinkō
ovulation	排卵	hairan
ovum	卵子	ranshi
owner 　　landlord	家主 大家	yanushi ōya

Chinese	Pin-yin	Wade-Giles
新生嬰兒死亡	xin sheng yinger si wang lü	hsin-sheng yinger szu-wang lü
因別死亡率	yin bie si wang lü	yin-pieh szu-wang lü
母語	mu yu	mu-yü
國家	guo jia	kuo-chia
祖籍	zu ji	tsu-chi
國籍	guo ji	kuo-chi
本國生	ben guo sheng	pen-kuo-sheng
自然區	zi ran qu	tzu-jan ch'ü
自然增加	zi ran zeng jia	tzu-jan tseng-chia
歸化	gui hua	kui-hua
純	chun	ch'un
遊牧	you mu	yu-mu
無答	wu da	wu ta
數目	shu mu	shu-mu
數字，圖表	shu zi, tu biao	shu-tzu, t'u-piao
整數	zheng shu	cheng-shu
婚姻	hun yin	hun-yin
職業	zhi ye	chih-yeh
後代	hou dai	hou-tai
老年	lao nian	lao-nien
過剩人口	guo sheng ren kou	kuo-sheng jen-k'ou
排卵	pai luan	p'ai-luan
卵子	luan zi	luan-tzu
所有者	suo you zhe	so-yu-chê
地主	di zhu	ti-chu

English	Japanese	Japanese Transliteration
parenthood	親であること	oyadearu koto
parents	両親	ryōshin
parity	出生パリティ	shusshō paritii
birth order	出生秩序(順位)	shusshō chitsujo (jun'i)
people (nation)	国民	kokumin
percentage	百分率	hyakubun-ritsu
percent	パーセント	pāsento

periodic abstinence. *See* rhythm method.

person. *See* individual.

person of no fixed abode. *See* vagrant.

pessary. *See* diaphragm.

pill. *See* contraceptive pill.

English	Japanese	Japanese Transliteration
population	人口	jinkō
population, agricultural	農業人口	nōgyō jinkō
farm population	農家人口	nōka jinkō
population, closed	封鎖人口	fūsa jinkō
population decline	人口減少	jinkō genshō
negative growth	マイナス人口増加	mainasu jinkō zōka
population, de facto	現在人口	genzai jinkō
enumerated population		
population, de jure	常住人口	jōjū jinkō
resident population		
population density	人口密度	jinkō mitsudo
population, economically active	活動人口	katsudō jinkō

population, enumerated. *See* population, de facto.

English	Japanese	Japanese Transliteration
population forecast	人口予測	jinkō yosoku
population growth	人口増加	jinkō zōka
population, mean	平均人口	heikin jinkō
population, open	開放人口	kaihō jinkō
population optimum	人口適度	jinkō tekido
optimum population	適度人口	tekido jinkō
population policy	人口政策	jinkō seisaku
population pressure	人口圧力	jinkō atsuryoku
population projection	人口推計	jinkō suikei
population pyramid	人口ピラミッド	jinkō piramiddo

Chinese	Pin-yin	Wade-Giles
父母身份	fu mu shen fen	fu-mu shen-fen
父母	fu mu	fu-mu
生序	sheng xu	sheng-hsü
胎次	tai ci	t'ai-tz'u
國人	guo ren	kuo-jen
百分比	bai fen bi	pai-fen pi
百分之…	bai fen zhi . . .	pai-fen chih . . .
人口	ren kou	jen-k'ou
農業人口	nong ye ren kou	nung-yeh jen-k'ou
務農人口	wu nong ren kou	wu-nung jen-k'ou
封閉人口	feng bi ren kou	feng-pi jen-k'ou
人口減低	ren kou jian di	jen-k'ou chien-ti
負數成長	fu shu cheng zhang	fu-shu ch'eng-chang
現住人口	xian zhu ren kou	hsien-chu jen-k'ou
查計人口	cha ji ren kou	ch'a-chi jen-k'ou
常住人口	chang zhu ren kou	ch'ang-chu jen-k'ou
居住人口	ju zhu ren kou	chü-chu jen-k'ou
人口密度	ren kou mi du	jen-k'ou mi-tu
勞動人口	lao dong ren kou	lao-tung jen-k'ou
人口預測	ren kou yu ce	jen-k'ou yü-ts'ê
人口增長	ren kou zeng zhang	jen-k'ou tseng-chang
平均人口	ping jun ren kou	p'ing-chün jen-k'ou
開放人口	kai fang ren kou	k'ai-fang jen-k'ou
適度人口	shi du ren kou	shih-tu jen-k'ou
人口政策	ren kou zheng ce	jen-k'ou cheng-ts'ê
人口壓力	ren kou ya li	jen-k'ou ya-li
人口預測	ren kou yu ce	jen-k'ou yü-ts'ê
人口金字塔	ren kou jin zi ta	jen-k'ou chin-tzu t'a

English	Japanese	Japanese Transliteration
population, quasi-stable	準安定人口	jun-antei jinkō
population register	人口登録	jinkō tōroku
population, resident. *See* population, de jure.		
population, stable	安定人口	antei jinkō
population, standard	標準人口	hyōjun jinkō
population, stationary	静止人口	seishi jinkō
population statistics	人口統計	jinkō tōkei
positive check	積極的抑制	sekkyokuteki yokusei
pregnancy gestation	妊娠	ninshin
prematurity (of births)	早産	sōzan
prevalence rate	有病率	yubyō-ritsu
preventive check moral restraint	予防的抑制 道徳的抑制	shōkyokuteki yokusei dōtokuteki yokusei
probability	確率	kakuritsu
probable length of life. *See* life, median length of.		
productivity	生産力 生産性	seisanryoku seisansei
progeny. *See* offspring.		
proportion	割合	wariai
provisional	仮の 仮定の	karino katei no
puberty	思春期	shishunki
public health	公衆衛生	kōshū eisei
punch, n.	穿孔	senkō
punch card	穿孔カード パンチ・カード	senkō kādo panchi kādo
questionnaire	質問紙	shitsumonshi
race, n.	人種	jinshu
radix (of a life table)	ラディックス 年齢階級(生命表の)	radikkusu nenrei kaikyū (seimeihyō no)
range	分布範囲 範囲	bunpu han'i han'i
rate	率	ritsu

Chinese	Pin-yin	Wade-Giles
準穩定人口	zhun wen ding ren kou	chun wen-ting jen-k'ou
人口登記	ren kou deng ji	jen-k'ou teng-chi
穩定人口	wen ding ren kou	wen-ting jen-k'ou
標準人口	biao zhun ren kou	piao-chun jen-k'ou
靜止人口	jing zhi ren kou	ching-chih jen-k'ou
人口統計	ren kou tong ji	jen-k'ou t'ung-chi
積極性抑制	ji ji xing yi zhi	chi-chi-hsing yi-chih
懷孕	huai yun	huai-yün
妊娠	ren shen	jen-shen
早產	zao chan	tsao-ch'an
流行率	liu xing lü	liu-hsing lü
防止性抑制	fang zhi xing yi zhi	fang-chih hsing yi-chih
道德節制	dao de jie zhi	tao-tê chieh-chih
可能率	ke neng lü	k'o-neng lü
生產能力，生產率	sheng chan neng li sheng chan lü	sheng-ch'ang neng li sheng-ch'an lü
生產力	sheng chan li*	sheng-ch'an li*
比例	bi li	pi-li
暫定的	zhan ding di	chan-ting-ti
青春期	qing chun qi	ch'ing-ch'un ch'i
公共衛生	gong gong wei sheng	kung-kung wei-sheng
打孔	da kong	ta-k'ung
打卡	da ka	ta k'a
調查表	diao cha biao	tiao-ch'a piao
種族	zhong zu	chung-tsu
基數（生命表）	ji shu (sheng ming biao)	chi-shu (sheng-ming piao)
全距	quan ju	ch'üan chü
率	lü	lü

*Productive forces.

75

English	Japanese	Japanese Transliteration
ratio	比	hi
refined figure	補正数字	hosei sūji
refugee	難民	nanmin
region. *See* area.		
registration	住民登録	jūmin tōroku
relationship (to head of household)	続き柄(世帯主に対する)	tsuzuki-gara (setai-nushi ni tai-suru)
relatives	親類	shinrui
kin	せき	inseki
religion	宗教	shūkyō
remarriage	再婚	saikon
remigration. *See* migration, return.		
reproduction	再生産	saiseisan
reproduction rate, gross	総再生産率	sō-saiseisan-ritsu
reproduction rate, net	純再生産率	jun-saiseisan-ritsu
residence. *See* dwelling unit.		
respondent (census)	回答者(国勢調査)	kaitōsha (kokusei chōsa)
revised	訂正された	teiseisareta
corrected	補正された	hoseisareta
rhythm method	リズム法	rizumuhō
periodic abstinence	周期法	shūkihō
risk	危険率	kiken-ritsu
chance		
rural	農村の	nōson no
salpingectomy	卵管切断	rankan setsudan
sample, n.	標本	hyōhon
sample, probability	確率標本	kakuritsu hyōhon
sample, representative	代表標本	daihyō hyōhon
sample survey	標本調査	hyōhon chōsa
sampling, n.	標本抽出 サンプリング	hyōhon chūshutsu sanpuringu
sampling, area	地域抽出法	chiiki chūshutsuhō
sampling, cluster	集落抽出法 クラスター・サンプリング	shūraku chūshutsuhō kurasutā sanpuringu
sampling error	標本誤差	hyōhon gosa
sampling, stratified	層化抽出法	sōka chūshutsuhō

Chinese	Pin-yin	Wade-Giles
比例	bi li	pi-li
精細數字	jing xi shu zi	ching-hsi shu-tzu
難民	nan min	nan-min
登記	deng ji	teng-chi
關係	guan xi	kuan-hsi
親屬	qin shu	ch'in-shu
宗教	zong jiao	tsung-chiao
再婚	zai hun	tsai-hun
繁殖	fan zhi	fan-chih
粗再生產率	cu zai sheng chan lü	tsu tsai sheng ch'an lü
淨再生產率	jing zai sheng chan zhi lü	ching tsai sheng ch'an lü
應答者	ying da zhe	ying-ta-chê
校正的	jiao zheng di	chiao cheng-ti
週期法	zhou qi fa	chou-ch'i fa
危險率	wei xian lü	wei-hsien lü
機會	ji hui	chi-hui
農村	nong cun	nung ts'un
輸卵管切除術	shu luan guan qie chu shu	shu-lüan-kuan ch'ieh-ch'u-shu
樣本	yang ben	yang-pen
機遇樣本	ji yu yang ben	chi-yü yang-pen
代表樣本	dai biao yang ben	tai-piao yang-pen
樣本調查	yang ben diao cha	yang-pen tiao-ch'a
選樣	xuan yang	hsüan-yang
抽樣	chou yang	ch'ou-yang
地區選樣	di qu xuan yang	ti-ch'ü hsüan-yang
集體選樣	ji ti xuan yang	chi-t'i hsüan-yang
整群抽樣	zheng qun chou yang	cheng-ch'ün ch'ou-yang
選樣誤差	xuan yang wu cha	hsüan-yang wu-ch'a
分層選樣	fen ceng xuan yang	fen-t'seng hsüan-yang

English	Japanese	Japanese Transliteration
scatter. *See* dispersion.		
schedule, n.	調査票	chōsahyō
segregation	隔離 分離	kakuri bunri
self-enumeration	自記式調査 自計式調査	jikishiki chōsa jikeishiki chōsa
senility	老齢	rōrei
series	系列	keiretsu
set, n.	組 セット	kumi setto
sex	性	sei
sex-age-specific rate	性年齢別特殊率	sei-nenrei-betsu-tokushu-ritsu
sex ratio	性比	seihi
sexual intercourse. *See* coitus.		
sheath. *See* condom.		
siblings	きょうだい	kyōdai
significance, level of	有意水準	yūi suijun
simulation	シミュレーション	shumirēshon
single never married	独身 単身 未婚	dokushin tanshin mikon
SMA. *See* standard metropolitan area.		
smoothing (of a curve)	平準化 平滑化	heijunka heikatsuka
social class	社会階級 社会階層	shakai kaikyū shakai kaisō
social mobility	社会移動	shakai idō
social stratification	社会成層	shakai seisō
socio-economic group	社会経済的集団	shakai-keizaiteki shūdan
sorter (machine)	分類機	bunruiki
soul. *See* individual.		
spacing (of births), n.	間隔(出生の)	kankaku (shusshō no)
spatial distribution. *See* geographical distribution.		
sperm	精液	seieki
spinster	未婚女子	mikon joshi
sponge (contraceptive)	スポンジ(避妊用具)	suponji (hinin yōgu)

Chinese	Pin-yin	Wade-Giles
調查表	diao cha biao	tiao-ch'a piao
訪問表	fang wen biao	fang-wen piao
隔離	ge li	ko-li
自我查計	zi wo cha ji	tzu-wo ch'a-chi
衰老	shuai lao	shuai-lao
數列	shu lie	shu-lieh
組	zu	tsu
性別	xing bie	hsing-pieh
性年別比率	xing nian bie bi lü	hsing nien pieh pi-lü
性比例	xing bi li	hsing pi li
兄弟姐妹	shou zu	shou-tsu
顯著度	xian zhu du	hsien-chu tu
模擬	mo ni	mo-ni
單身	dan shen	tan shen
未婚	wei hun	wei hun
均勻化	jun yun hua	chün-yün hua
社會階級	she hui jie ji	shê-hui chieh-chi
社會流動	she hui liu dong	shê-hui liu-tung
社會階層	she hui jie ceng	shê-hui chieh-ts'eng
社會經濟團體	she hui jing ji tuan ti	shê-hui ching-chi t'uan-t'i
歸類機	qui lei ji	kui-lei chi
間隔	jian ge	chien-ke
精子	jing zi	ching-tzu
老處女	lao chu nü	lao ch'u-nü
海綿	hai mian	hai-mien

English	Japanese	Japanese Transliteration
spouse	配偶者	haigūsha
squatter	不法居住者	fuhō kyojūsha
	スクウォーター	sukuwōtā
standard deviation	標準偏差	hyōjun hensa
standard error	標準誤差	hyōjun gosa
standard metropolitan area agglomeration conurbation	標準大都市圏	hyōjun daitoshiken
standard of living. *See* living, level of.		
standardization, direct method of	直接標準化法	chokusetsu hyōjunkahō
standardization, indirect method of	間接標準化法	kansetsu hyōjunkahō
standardized (of a rate)	標準化(率)	hyōjunka (ritsu)
state, n.	国家	kokka
sterility infecundity	不妊(症)	funinshō
sterilization	不妊手術	funin shujutsu
stillbirth	死産	shizan
subject, n.	被調査者	hichōsasha
	調査客体	chōsa kyakutai
subpopulation	副次母集団	fukuji boshūdan
subsample	副標本	fuku hyōhon
subsistence level	生活維持水準	seikatsu iji suijun
suburb	郊外	kōgai
survey, n.	調査	chōsa
	踏査	tōsa
	サーベイ	sābei
survival, probability of	生存率	seizon-ritsu
	生残率	seizan-ritsu
survivor	生存者	seizonsha
table, n.	表	hyō
tabulate	集計する	shūkei suru
	製表する	seihyō suru
tabulation, cross-	クロス集計	kurosu shūkei
tenant	借家人	shakuyanin
	借地人	shakuchinin
territory. *See* area.		
time series	時系列	jikeiretsu

Chinese	Pin-yin	Wade-Giles
配偶	pei ou	p'ei-ou
違障居民	wei zhang ju min	wei-chang chü-min
標準偏差	biao zhun pian cha	piao-chun p'ien-ch'a
標準誤差	biao zhun wu cha	piao-chun wu-ch'a
標準都會區	biao zhun du hui qu	piao-chun tu-hui ch'ü
直接法標準化	zhi jie fa biao zhun hua	chih-chieh fa piao-chun hua
間接法標準化	jian jie fa biao zhun hua	chien-chieh fa piao-chun hua
標準化	biao zhun hua	piao-chun hua
國家	guo jia	kuo-chia
不妊	bu ren	pu-jen
絶育	jue yu	chüeh-yü
死產	si chan	szu-ch'an
被調查的對象	bei diao cha de dui xiang	pei tiao-ch'a te tui-hsiang
次人口	ci ren kou	tz'u jen-k'ou
次樣本	ci yang ben	tz'u yang-pen
生計度	sheng ji du	sheng chi tu
市郊	shi jiao	shih-chiao
調查	diao cha	tiao-ch'a
存活概率	cun huo gai lü	ts'un-huo kai-lü
存活者	cun huo zhe	ts'un-huo che
表	biao	piao
列表	lie biao	lieh piao
交互列表	jiao hu lie biao	chiao hu lieh piao
租户	zu hu	tsu-hu
時間數列	shi jian shu lie	shih-chien shu-lieh

English	Japanese	Japanese Transliteration
total years lived	生存年数	seizon nensū
town. *See* city.		
transient, n.	短期滞在者 一時現住者	tanki taizaisha ichiji genjūsha
trend	動向 傾向変動 トレンド	dōkō keikō hendō torendo
true rate. *See* intrinsic rate.		
tubal ligation	卵管結紮	rankan kessatsu
underdeveloped country. *See* less developed country.		
underenumeration	過少評価(調査結果の)	kashō hyōka (chōsa kekka no)
underpopulation	過少人口	kashō jinkō
underregistration	登録人口の調査漏れ 過少登録	tōroku jinkō no chōsa more kashō tōroku
unemployed, adj.	失業中の	shitsugyō chū no
unemployed, n.	失業者	shitsugyōsha
union	結婚 同棲	kekkon dōsei
union, consensual	同意婚	dōikon
union, free concubinage	自由婚 めかけ関係	jiyūkon mekake kankei
unknown not stated	不明	fumei
unmarried person. *See* bachelor; single; spinster.		
urban	都市の	toshi no
urbanization	都市化	toshika
uterus womb	子宮	shikyū
vagrant person of no fixed abode	放浪者 住所不定者	hōrōsha jūsho futeishā
variable, n.	変数	hensū
variation variability	変異 変動 変異性 可変性	hen'i hendō hen'isei kahensei
vasectomy	精管切除手術	seikan setsujo shujutsu
viable (of a fetus)	生命力のある(胎児が)	seimeiryoku no aru (taiji ga)

Chinese	Pin-yin	Wade-Giles
生存總年數	sheng cun zhong nian shu	sheng-ts'un tsung nien shu
過客	guo ke	kuo-k'o
趨勢	qu shi	ch'ü-shih
輸卵管結紮	shu luan guan jie zha	shu-lüan-kuan chieh-cha
查計偏低	cha ji pian di	ch'a-chi p'ien-ti
人口偏低	ren kou pian di	jen-k'ou p'ien-ti
登記過低	deng ji guo di	teng-chi kuo-ti
無業	wu ye	wu-yeh
無業者	wu ye zhe	wu-yeh-chê
結合	jie he	chieh-ho
情願結合	qing yuan jie he	ch'ing-yüan chieh-ho
自由結合	zi you jie he	tzu-yu chieh-ho
姘居	pin ju	p'ing chü
情況不明無答	qing kuang bu ming wu da	ch'ing-k'uang pu-ming wu ta
城鎮	cheng zhen	ch'eng-chen
都市化	du shi hua	tu-shih hua
子宮	zi gong	tzu-kung
流浪者	liu lang zhe	liu-lang-chê
變數	bian shu	pien-shu
變異	bian yi	pien i
輸精管切除術	shu jing quan qie chu shu	shu-ching-kuan ch'ieh-ch'u-shu
可育的(胎兒)	ke yu di (tai er)	k'o yü-ti (t'ai-erh)

English	Japanese	Japanese Transliteration
village	村	mura
vital revolution. *See* demographic transition.		
vital statistics	人口動態統計	jinkō dōtai tōkei
weight (statistical)	加重値	kajūchi
weighted mean weighted average	加重平均	kajū heikin
withdrawal. *See* coitus interruptus.		
woman. *See* female, n.		
womb. *See* uterus.		
younging (of a population)	若年化(人口の)	jakunenka (jinkō no)

Chinese	Pin-yin	Wade-Giles
鄉村	xiang cun	hsiang-ts'un
生命統計	sheng ming tong ji	sheng-ming t'ung-chi
權數	quan shu	ch'üan-shu
加權平均數	jia quan ping jun shu	chia-ch'üang p'ing-chün shu
年青化	nian qing hua	nien-ch'ing hua

English-Russian

abortion	аборт	abort
abortion, induced	искусственный аборт	iskusstvennyi abort
abortion, spontaneous miscarriage	непреднамеренный аборт непроизвольный аборт выкидыш	neprednamerennyi abort neproizvol'nyi abort vykidysh
acculturation	приобщение к культуре	priobschenie k kul'ture
accuracy	достоверность	dostovernost'
adolescence	юность	iunost'
adolescent, n.	юноша девушка	iunosha, m. devushka, f.
adult, n.	взрослый	vzroslyi
age	возраст	vozrast

age distribution
    age structure
	возрастной состав
	возрастная структура
	   населения
		vozrastnoi sostav
		vozrastnaia struktura naseleniia

age group(ing) age bracket	возрастная группировка возрастная группа	vozrastnaia gruppirovka vozrastnaia gruppa
age-specific rate	повозрастной коэффициент	povozrastnyi koeffitsient
agglomeration. *See* standard metropolitan area.		
aging, n.	старение	starenie
alien, n.	иностранец	inostranets
analysis	анализ	analiz

area
    territory
    region
	площадь
	территория
	район
	регион
		ploshchad'
		territoriia
		raion
		region

arrival (of immigrants)	прибытие	pribytie
assimilation	ассимиляция	assimilatsiia
attribute. *See* characteristic.		
average. *See* mean, adj.; mean, n.		
baby. *See* infant.		
bachelor	неженатый не состоящий в браке	nezhenatyi ne sostoiashchii v brake
base, n.	база	baza
birth	рождение	rozhdenie
birth control	регулирование деторождения контроль рождаемости	regulirovanie detorozhdeniia kontrol' rozhdaemosti

birth interval	интервал между рождениями интергенетический интервал	interval mezhdu rozhdeniiami intergeneticheskii interval
birth, live	живорождение	zhivorozhdenie
birth, multiple	многоплодные роды	mnogoplodnye rody
birth order. *See* parity.		
birth, premature	недоношенное рождение	nedonoshennoe rozhdenie
birth rate	коэффициент рождаемости	koeffitsient rozhdaemosti
block, n.	квартал	kvartal
boarder lodger	живущий в пансионе жилец	zhivushchii v pansione zhilets
bunching. *See* heaping.		
capital (city)	столица	stolitsa
celibacy	безбрачие	bezbrachie
census	перепись	perepis'
census tract	переписной район	perepisnoi raion
central city	центральный город	tsentral'nyi gorod
cervical cap. *See* diaphragm.		
chance. *See* risk.		
characteristic attribute	качественный признак характеристика качество свойство	kachestvennyi priznak kharakteristika kachestvo svoistvo

child-woman ratio	отношение числа детей к
	    числу матерей
	детность
		otnoshenie chisla detei k chislu
		    materei
		detnost'

citizen	гражданин	grazhdanin
city town	город городок	gorod gorodok
civil status. *See* marital status.		
classify	классифицировать	klassifitsirovat'
climacteric. *See* menopause.		
code, v.	шифровать по коду	shifrovat' po kodu kodirovat'
cohabitation. *See* coitus.		
cohort	когорта	kogorta
cohort fertility. *See* fertility.		

English		Russian
cohort, synthetic	синтетическая когорта	sinteticheskaia kogorta
coitus	койтус	koĭtus
sexual intercourse	половое сношение	polovoe snoshenie
cohabitation	сожительство	sozhitel'stvo
coitus interruptus	прерванное сношение	prervannoe snoshenie
withdrawal		
color (of skin)	цвет	tsvet
commuter	лицо, совершающее регулярные поездки	litso, sovershaiushchee reguli nye poezdki
commuting	маятниковая миграция	maiatnikovaia migratsiia
computer (electronic)	электронно-вычислительная машина	elektronno-vychislitel'naia ma shina
	ЭВМ	EVM
conception	зачатие	zachatie
concubinage. *See* union.		
condom	презерватив	prezervativ
sheath		
conjugal status. *See* marital status.		
contraception	пользование противозачаточными средствами	pol'zovanie protivozacha chnymi sredstvami
contraceptive, n.	противозачаточное средство	protivozachatochnoe sredstvo
contraceptive method	способ предупреждения зачатия	sposob preduprezhdeniia zacł tiia
contraceptive, oral	противозачаточные средства для внутреннего приема	protivozachatochnye sredstva d vnutrennego priema
contraceptive pill	противозачаточные таблетки	protivozachatochnye tabletki
contraceptive, postcoital	противозачаточные средства, принимаемые после сношения	protivozachatochnye sredstva, prinimaemye posle snosheni
morning-after pill		
conurbation. *See* standard metropolitan area.		
corrected. *See* revised.		
count, n.	счет	schet
	подсчет	podschet
	учет	uchet
country	страна	strana
couple (married)	пара (супружеская)	para (supruzheskaia)
cross-tabulation. *See* tabulation, cross.		

English	Russian	
crude (of a rate)	общий (коэффициент)	obshchii (koeffitsient)
data	статистические данные	statisticheskie dannye
data, basic	основные данные	osnovnye dannye
crude data	общие данные	obshchie dannye
primary data	первичные данные	pervichnye dannye
raw data	необработанные данные	neobrabotannye dannye
death	смерть	smert'
death, cause of	причина смерти	prichina smerti
death certificate	свидетельство о смерти	svidetel'stvo o smerti
death, probability of	вероятность смерти	veroiatnost' smerti
death rate	коэффициент смертности	koeffitsient smertnosti
demographer	демограф	demograf
demographic transition	демографический переход	demograficheskii perekhod
demographic revolution	демографическая революция	demograficheskaia revoliutsiia
demography	демография	demografiia
denomination (religious)	вероисповедание	veroispovedanie
departure (of emigrants)	отъезд	ot'ezd
dependency ratio	отношение числа иждивенцев к числу работающих	otnoshenie chisla izhdiventsev k chislu rabotaiushchikh
dependent, n.	иждивенец	izhdivenets
dependent children	дети, находящиеся на иждивении	deti, nakhodiashchiesia na izhdivenii
depopulation	депопуляция	depopuliatsiia
diagram	диаграмма	diagramma
graph	график	grafik
diaphragm	диафрагма	diafragma
cervical cap	колпачек	kolpachok
pessary		
difference	различие	razlichie
disability	нетрудоспособность временная утрата трудоспособности	netrudosposobnost' vremennaia utrata trudosposobnosti
disease	заболевание	zabolevanie
dispersion	дисперсия	dispersiia
scatter, n.		
displaced person	перемещенное лицо	peremeshchennoe litso
distribution (frequency)	распределение	raspredelenie

divorce	развод	razvod
dwelling unit residence	жилище местожительство	zhilishche mestozhitel'stvo
ecology, human	экология человека	ekologiia cheloveka
economic development economic growth	экономическое развитие	ekonomicheskoe razvitie
economic sector. *See* industry.		
education, higher	высшее образование	vysshee obrazovanie
education, primary	начальное образование	nachal'noe obrazovanie
education, secondary	среднее образование	srednee obrazovanie
emigration	эмиграция	emigratsiia
employed	имеющий работу занятый	imeiushchii rabotu zaniatyi
endogenous (of a death)	органическая (смертность) эндогенная (смертность)	organicheskaia (smertnost') endogennaia (smertnost')
enumeration	перечисление учет	perechislenie uchet
enumerator	счетчик регистратор	schetchik registrator
epidemic, n.	эпидемия	epidemiia
estimate, n. estimation	оценка	otsenka
estimate, v.	оценивать	otsenivat'
ethnic group	этническая группа	etnicheskaia gruppa
eugenics	евгеника	evgenika
ever married, adj.	лица, когда-либо состоявшие в браке	litsa, kogda-libo sostoiavshie v brake
exogenous (of a death)	неорганическая (смертность) экзогенная (смертность)	neorganicheskaia (smertnost') ekzogennaia (smertnost')
expectation of life. *See* life expectancy.		
extrapolation	экстраполяция	ekstrapoliatsiia
family	семья	sem'ia
family allowance family subsidy	пособие семьям	posobie sem'iam
family, nuclear	нуклеарная семья	nuklearnaia sem'ia
family planning	регулирование размеров семьи	regulirovanie razmerov sem'i

English		
family size	размеры семьи	razmery sem'i
farm population. *See* population, agricultural.		
fecundability	способность к зачатию	sposobnost' k zachatiiu
fecundity	потенциальная плодовитость	potentsial'naia plodovitost'
female, n.	лицо женского пола	litso zhenskogo pola
woman	женщина	zhenshchina
fertility	плодовитость	plodovitost'
natality	рождаемость	rozhdaemost'
fertility, cohort	плодовитость когорты	plodovitost' kogorty
fertility, completed	исчерпанная плодовитость	ischerpannaia plodovitost'
fertility rate	коэффициент плодовитости	koeffitsient plodovitosti
fertility rate, total	суммарный коэффициент плодовитости	summarnyi koeffitsient plodovitosti
fertilization	оплодотворение	oplodotvorenie
fetus	утробный плод	utrobnyi plod
	фетус	fetus
figure. *See* number.		
fluctuation	колебание	kolebanie
	флуктуация	fluktuatsiia
follow-up, n.	повторная рассылка переписных листов	povtornaia rassylka perepisnykh listov
foreign-born	родившийся в другой стране	rodivshiisia v drugoi strane
form, n.	форма	forma
generation	поколение	pokolenie
generation, length of a	длина поколения	dlina pokoleniia
genetics	генетика	genetika
geographical distribution	территориальное распределение	territorial'noe raspredelenie
spatial distribution		
geographical mobility	географическая мобильность	geograficheskaia mobil'nost'
spatial mobility	территориальная мобильность	territorial'naia mobil'nost'
geometric mean	средняя геометрическая	sredniaia geometricheskaia
geriatrics	гериатрия	geriatriia
gerontology	геронтология	gerontologiia
gestation. *See* pregnancy.		
graph. *See* diagram.		

English	Russian	
gross	брутто	brutto
group	группа	gruppa
hamlet	хутор	khutor
	выселки	vyselki
head. *See* household.		
heaping bunching	аккумуляция	akkumuliatsiia
heredity	наследственность	nasledstvennost'
household	двор	dvor
	домохозяйство	domokhoziaistvo
household, head of a	домохозяин	domokhoziain
	глава семьи	glava sem'i
household, member of a	член домохозяйства	chlen domokhoziaistva
illegitimacy	незаконное рождение	nezakonnoe rozhdenie
illegitimate	незаконорожденный	nezakonnorozhdennyi
immigration	иммиграция	immigratsiia
incidence rate	коэффициент частоты (заболеваний)	koeffitsient chastoty (zabolev\ nii)
index	индекс	indeks
indicator	показатель	pokazatel'
individual person soul	человек лицо душа	chelovek litso dusha
industry sector of the economy	промышленность отрасль (народного) хозяйства	promyshlennost' otrasl' (narodnogo) khoziaistva
infant baby	младенец ребенок	mladenets rebenok
infecundity. *See* sterility.		
inhabitant	житель	zhitel'
interpolation	интерполяция	interpoliatsiia
interviewer	счетчик	schetchik
intra-uterine device IUD	внутриматочные противозачаточные средства	vnutrimatochnye protivozacha- tochnye sredstva
intrinsic rate true rate	истинный коэффициент	istinnyi koeffitsient
IUD. *See* intra-uterine device.		
kin. *See* relatives.		

lactation (prolonged)	(удлиненное грудное) кормление	(udlinennoe grudnoe) kormlenie
landlord. *See* owner.		
language, native. *See* mother tongue.		
legitimacy	законность	zakonnost'
legitimate	законнорожденный	zakonnorozhdennyi
length of life. *See* longevity.		
less developed country underdeveloped country	развивающаяся страна малоразвитая страна	razvivaiushchaiasia strana malorazvitaia strana
life expectancy expectation of life	средняя продолжительность предстоящей жизни	sredniaia prodolzhitel'nost' predstoiashchei zhizni
life expectancy at birth	средняя продолжительность жизни при рождении	sredniaia prodolzhitel'nost' zhizni pri rozhdenii
mean length of life	средняя продолжительность жизни	sredniaia prodolzhitel'nost' zhizni
life, median length of	среднее число человеко-лет, прожитых исходной массой	srednee chislo cheloveko-let, prozhitykh iskhodnoi massoi
probable length of life	вероятная продолжительность предстоящей жизни	veroiatnaia prodolzhitel'nost' predstoiashchei zhizni
life span	прожитые годы жизни	prozhitye gody zhizni
life table mortality table	таблицы смертности	tablitsy smertnosti
life table, abridged	сокращенные таблицы смертности	sokrashchennye tablitsy smertnosti
life table, complete	полные таблицы смертности	polnye tablitsy smertnosti
literate person	грамотный человек	gramotnyi chelovek
living, level of standard of living	уровень жизни жизненный уровень	uroven' zhizni zhiznennyi uroven'
lodger. *See* boarder.		
longevity length of life	продолжительность жизни	prodolzhitel'nost' zhizni
male, n. man	лицо мужского пола человек мужчина	litso muzhskogo pola chelovek muzhchina
marital status civil status conjugal status	семейное положение	semeinoe polozhenie
marriage	брак	brak

marriage, common-law. *See* union, consensual.

marriage, duration of	продолжительность брака	prodolzhitel'nost' braka
marriage rate	коэффициент брачности	koeffitsient brachnosti
married man	женатый человек	zhenatyi chelovek
married woman	замужняя женщина	zamuzhniaia zhenshchina
mean, adj. average, adj.	средний	srednii
mean, n. average, n.	средняя величина	sredniaia velichina
mean deviation	среднее отклонение	srednee otklonenie

mean length of life. *See* life expectancy at birth.

median, adj.	медианный	mediannyi
median, n.	медиана	mediana

median length of life. *See* life, median length of.

menarche	менархе	menarkhe
menopause climacteric	менопауза климакс	menopauza klimaks
menstrual cycle	менструальный цикл	menstrual'nyi tsikl
menstruation	менструация	menstruatsiia
migrant	мигрант	migrant
migration	миграция	migratsiia
migration, forced	принудительная миграция	prinuditel'naia migratsiia
migration, internal	внутренняя миграция	vnutrenniaia migratsiia
migration, international	международная миграция	mezhdunarodnaia migratsiia
migration, net	нетто-миграция	netto-migratsiia
migration, return remigration	обратная миграция	obratnaia migratsiia
minority	меньшинство	men'shinstvo

miscarriage. *See* abortion.

mobility. *See* geographical mobility; social mobility.

modal	модальный	modal'nyi
mode	мод форма	mod forma
model, n.	модель	model'

moral restraint. *See* preventive check.

morbidity	заболеваемость	zabolevaemost'

English	Russian	
mortality	смертность	smertnost'
mortality, differential	различия в смертности	razlichiia v smertnosti
mortality, fetal	внутриутробная смертнодть	vnutriutrobnaia smertnost'
mortality, infant	детская смертность	detskaia smertnost'
mortality, maternal puerperal mortality	материнская смертность	materinskaia smertnost'
mortality, neonatal	ранняя детская смертность смертность новорожденных	ranniaia detskaia smertnost' smertnost' novorozhdennykh
mortality, perinatal	перинатальная смертность	perinatal'naia smertnost'
mortality, post-neonatal	детская смертность на первом году жизни в возрасте старше одного месяца	detskaia smertnost' na pervoı godu zhizni v vozraste starsł odnogo mesiatsa
mortality rate. *See* death rate.		
mortality rate, cause-specific	коэффициент смертности от определенных причин	koeffitsient smertnosti ot opro delennykh prichin
mortality table. *See* life table.		
mother tongue native language	родной язык	rodnoi iazyk
natality. *See* fertility.		
nation	нация	natsiia
national origin	национальное происхождение	natsional'noe proiskhozhdenie
nationality	национальность	natsional'nost'
native-born	местный уроженец	mestnyi urozhenets
native language. *See* mother tongue.		
natural area	ареал область географического распространения	areal oblast' geograficheskogo raspro straneniia
natural increase	естественный прирост	estestvennyi prirost
naturalization	натурализация	naturalizatsiia
negative growth. *See* population decline.		
net	нетто-	netto-
never-married. *See* single.		
nomad	кочевник	kochevnik
nonresponse	лицо, не сообщившее сведений	litso, ne soobshchivshee sveder
not stated. *See* unknown.		

English	Russian	
number, n. figure, n.	число	chislo
number, round	округленное число	okruglennoe chislo
nuptiality	брачность	brachnost'
occupation	занятие профессия	zaniatie professiia
offspring progeny	потомство	potomstvo
old age	старость	starost'
overpopulation	перенаселение	perenaselenie
ovulation	овуляция	ovuliatsiia
ovum	яйцо	iaitso
owner landlord	владелец хозяин дома	vladelets khoziain doma
parenthood (fatherhood, mother- hood)	отцовство, материнство	ottsovstvo, materinstvo
parents	родители	roditeli
parity birth order	число детей порядок родов немер рождения	chislo detei poriadok rodov nomer rozhdeniia
people (nation)	народ	narod
percentage percent	процент	protsent

periodic abstinence. *See* rhythm method.

person. *See* individual.

person of no fixed abode. *See* vagrant.

pessary. *See* diaphragm.

pill. *See* contraceptive pill.

population	население	naselenie
population, economically active	самодеятельное население	samodeiatel'noe naselenie
population, agricultural	сельскохозяйственное население	sel'skokhoziaistvennoe naselenie
rural population	сельское население	sel'skoe naselenie
population, closed	закрытое население замкнутое население	zakrytoe naselenie zamknutoe naselenie
population decline negative growth	убыль населения отрицательный прирост	ubyl' naseleniia otritsatel'nyi prirost
population, de facto enumerated population	фактическое население наличное население	fakticheskoe naselenie nalichnoe naselenie

population, de jure	юридическое население	iuridicheskoe naselenie
resident population	постоянное население	postoiannoe naselenie
population density	показатель плотности населения	pokazatel' plotnosti naseleniia

population, enumerated. *See* population, de facto.

population forecast	перспективное исчисление населения	perspektivnoe ischislenie naseleniia
population growth	рост населения	rost naseleniia
population, mean	среднее население	srednee naselenie
population, open	открытое население	otkrytoe naselenie
population optimum	оптимальная численность населения	optimal'naia chislennost' naseleniia
optimum population	оптимум населения	optimum naseleniia
population policy	демографическая политика	demograficheskaia politika
population pressure	демографическое давление	demograficheskoe davlenie
population projection	прогноз населения	prognoz naseleniia
population pyramid	возрастно-половая пирамида	vozrastno-polovaia piramida
population, quasi-stable	квази-стабильное население	kvazi-stabil'noe naselenie
population register	списки населения	spiski naseleniia

population, resident. *See* population, de jure.

population, stable	стабильное население	stabil'noe naselenie
population, standard	стандартное население	standartnoe naselenie
population, stationary	стационарное население	statsionarnoe naselenie
population statistics	демографическая статистика	demograficheskaia statistika
positive check	положительная проверка	polozhitel'naia proverka
pregnancy	беременность	beremennost'
gestation	длительность беременности	dlitel'nost' beremennosti
prematurity (of births)	недоношенность (родов)	nedonoshennost' (rodov)
prevalence rate	процент больных	protsent bol'nykh
preventive check	превентивная проверка	preventivnaia proverka
moral restraint	предупредительные меры	predupreditel'nye mery
probability	вероятность	veroiatnost'

probable length of life. *See* life, median length of.

productivity	производительность	proizvoditel'nost'

progeny. *See* offspring.

proportion	пропорция	proportsiia
provisional	предварительный	predvariatel'nyi

puberty	половая зрелость	polovaia zrelost'
public health	здравоохранение	zdravookhranenie
punch, n.	перфорационная карточка	perforatsiia
punch card	перфорационная карточка	perforatsionnaia kartochka
questionnaire	анкета	anketa
	вопросник	voprosnik
race, n.	раса	rasa
radix (of a life table)	исходная совокупность родившихся	iskhodnaia sovokupnost' rodi shikhsia
range	размах	razmakh
rate	коэффициент	koeffitsient
ratio	отношение	otnoshenie
refined data	обработанные данные	obrabotannye dannye
refugee	беженец	bezhenets
region. *See* area.		
registration	регистрация	registratsiia
relationship (to head of household)	отношение (к главе семьи)	otnoshenie (k glave sem'i)
relatives	родственники	rodstvenniki
kin	род	rod
religion	вера	vera
	религия	religiia
remarriage	вступление в новый брак	vstuplenie v novyi brak
	повторный брак	povtornyi brak
remigration. *See* migration, return.		
reproduction	воспроизводство	vosproizvodstvo
reproduction rate, gross	брутто-коэффициент воспроизводства	brutto-koeffitsient vosproizvod stva
reproduction rate, net	нэтто-коэффициент воспроизводства	netto-koeffitsient vosproizvod stva
residence. *See* dwelling unit.		
respondent (census)	опрашиваемое лицо	oprashivaemoe litso
revised	пересмотренный	peresmotrennyi
corrected	исправленный	ispravlennyi
rhythm method	календарный метод	kalendarnyi metod
	биологический ритм	biologicheskii ritm
periodic abstinence	периодическое воздержание	periodicheskoe vozderzhanie

English	Russian	
risk	риск	risk
chance	возможность	vozmozhnost'
rural	сельское	sel'skoe
salpingectomy	перевязывание маточных придатков	pereviazyvanie matochnykh pridatkov
sample, n.	выборка	vyborka
sample, probability	вероятностная (взвешенная) выборка	veroiatnostnaia (vzveshennaia) vyborka
sample, representative	репрезентативная выборка	reprezentativnaia vyborka
sample survey	выборочное обследование	vyborochnoe obsledovanie
sampling, n.	выборочный метод	vyborochnyi metod
sampling, area	территориальная выборка	territorial'naia vyborka
sampling, cluster	групповая выборка	gruppovaia vyborka
sampling error	ошибка выборки	oshibka vyborki
sampling, stratified	типологическая выборка	tipologicheskaia vyborka
scatter. *See* dispersion.		
schedule, n.	переписной лист структура расписание	perepisnoi list struktura raspisanie
segregation	сегрегация	segregatsiia
self-enumeration	самоисчисление	samoischislenie
senility	сенильность	senil'nost'
series	серия	seriia
set, n.	ряд	riad
sex	пол	pol
sex-age-specific rate	поло-возрастные коэффициенты	polo-vozrastnye koeffitsienty
sex ratio	соотношение полов	sootnoshenie polov
sexual intercourse. *See* coitus.		
sheath. *See* condom.		
siblings	родные (братья и сестры)	rodnye (brat'ia i sestry)
significance, level of	уровень значимости	uroven' znachimosti
simulation	симуляция	simuliatsiia
single	одинокие	odinokie
never married	никогда не состоявшие в браке	nikogda ne sostoiavshie v brake

101

SMA. *See* standard metropolitan area.

smoothing (of a curve)	выравнивание	vyravnivanie
social class	общественный класс	obshchestvennyi klass
social mobility	социальная мобильность изменение классового состава	sotsial'naia mobil'nost' izmenenie klassovogo sostava
social stratification	социальная стратификация	sotsial'naia stratifikatsiia
socio-economic group	социально-экономическая группа	sotsial'no-ekonomicheskaia gruppa
sorter (machine)	сортировщик	sortirovshchik

soul. *See* individual.

spacing (of births), n.	регулирование интервалов между рождениями	regulirovanie intervalov mezhd rozhdeniiami

spatial distribution. *See* geographical distribution.

sperm	сперма	sperma
spinster	девица	devitsa
sponge (contraceptive)	тампон	tampon
spouse	супруг, супруга	suprug, supruga
squatter	сквоттер	skvatter
standard deviation	среднеквадратическое отклонение	srednekvadraticheskoe otklo-nenie
standard error	стандартная ошибка	standartnaia oshibka
standard metropolitan area	условный статистический район большого города с пригородами	uslovnyi statisticheskii raion bol' shogo goroda s prigorodami
agglomeration conurbation	городская агломерация конурбация	gorodskaia aglomeratsiia konurbatsiia

standard of living. *See* living, level of.

standardization, direct method of	прямой метод стандартизации	priamoi metod standartizatsii
standardization, indirect method of	косвенный метод стандартизации	kosvennyi metod standartizatsii
standardized (of a rate)	стандартизованный	standartizovannyi
state, n.	государство	gosudarstvo
sterility infecundity	стерильность бесплодие	steril'nost' besplodie
sterilization	стерилизация	sterilizatsiia

English	Russian	
stillbirth	мертворождение	mertvorozdenie
subject, n.	подданный	poddanyi
subpopulation	подгруппа населения	podgruppa naseleniia
subsample	подвыборка	podvyborka
subsistence level	прожиточный минимум	prozhitochnyi minimum
suburb	пригород	prigorod
survey, n.	обследование	obsledovanie
survival, probability of	вероятность дожития	veroiatnost' dozhitiia
survivor	доживающий	dozhivaiushchii
table, n.	таблица	tablitsa
tabulate	табулировать	tabulirovat'
tabulation, cross-	комбинационные таблицы	kombinatsionnye tablitsy
tenant	наниматель (жилого помещения)	nanimatel' (zhilogo pome-shcheniia)
territory. *See* area.		
time series	динамический ряд временный ряд	dinamicheskii riad vremennyi riad
total years lived	сумма человеко-лет	summa cheloveko-let
town. *See* city.		
transient, n.	временно проживающий	vremenno prozhivaiushchii
trend	тенденция динамика	tendentsiia dinamika
true rate. *See* intrinsic rate.		
tubal ligation	перевязывание маточных труб	pereviazyvanie matochnykh trub
underdeveloped country. *See* less developed country.		
underenumeration	недоучет численности населения	nedouchet chislennosti naseleniia
underpopulation	недостаточная населенность	nedostatochnaia naselennost'
underregistration	неполная регистрация	nepolnaia registratsiia
unemployed, adj.	безработный незанятый	bezrabotnyi nezaniatyi
unemployed, n.	безработные	bezrabotnye
union	брачный союз	brachnyi soiuz
union, consensual	гражданский брак	grazhdanskii brak

English	Russian	
union, free concubinage	фактический брак внебрачное сожительство	faktisheskii brak vnebrachnoe sozhitel'stvo

unknown
    not stated
	не указан
	вопросы, оставленные без
	    ответа
		ne ukazan
		voprosy, ostavlennye bez otvet

unmarried person. *See* bachelor; single; spinster.		
urban	городское	gorodskoe
urbanization	урбанизация	urbanizatsiia
uterus womb	матка	matka

vagrant
    person of no fixed abode
	лицо, не имеющее
	    постоянного
	    местожительства
		litso, ne imeiushchee postoian
		    nogo mestozhitel'stva

variable, n.	переменная	peremennaia
variation variability	вариация	variatsiia
vasectomy	васектомия	vasektomiia
viable (of a fetus)	жизнеспособный	zhiznesposobnyi
village	село	selo

vital statistics	данные о естественном
	    движении населения
		dannye o estestvennom dvizhen
		    naseleniia

weight (statistical)	вес	ves
weighted mean weighted average	взвешенная средняя	vzveshennaia sredniaia
withdrawal. *See* coitus interruptus.		
woman. *See* female, n.		
womb. *See* uterus.		
younging (of a population)	омоложение населения	omolozhenie naseleniia

French to English

French	English
accouchement	birth
accouchement avant terme	premature birth
accouchement gémellaire	multiple birth
accouchement multiple	multiple birth
accouchement prématuré	premature birth
d'accouchement, rang	birth order; parity
accroissement de la population	population growth
accroissement naturel	natural increase
accroissement négatif	negative growth; population decline
acculturation	acculturation
d'activité économique, branche	sector of the economy
d'activité économique, secteur	sector of the economy
adolescence	adolescence
adolescent	adolescent, m.
adulte	adult, n.
âge	age
l'âge atteint, taux selon	age-specific rate
âge, composition par	age distribution; age structure
âge, structure par	age structure; age distribution
âge, taux par	age-specific rate
d'âges, groupe	age group
âges, pyramide des	population pyramid
âges ronds, attraction des	heaping; bunching
agglomération (multicommunale)	standard metropolitan area
agglomération urbaine	urban place; conurbation; standard metropolitan area
l'agriculture, population vivant de	farm population; agricultural population
aire naturelle	natural area
ajustement	smoothing (of a curve)
allaitement (prolongé)	(prolonged) lactation
allocation familiale	family allowance; family subsidy
alphabète	literate person
âme	soul; individual
analyse	analysis

French	English
années vécues, nombre des	total years lived
anticonceptionnelle, méthode	contraceptive method
apparentés	relatives; kin
arrivée	arrival (of immigrants)
assimilation	assimilation
attraction des âges ronds	heaping; bunching
attraction des nombres ronds	heaping; bunching
autodénombrement	self-enumeration
autorecensement	self-enumeration
avortement	abortion
avortement provoqué	induced abortion
avortement spontané	spontaneous abortion
balance migratoire	net migration
banlieue	suburb
base	base, n.
bébé	baby
branche d'activité économique	industry
brut	crude (of a rate); gross
bulletin	schedule of a survey
bulletin de décès	death certificate
cape (cervicale)	diaphragm; pessary
capitale	capital (city)
caractère qualitatif	characteristic; attribute
carte mécanographique	punch card
carte perforée	punch card
catégorie sociale	socio-economic group
cause de décès	cause of death
célibat	celibacy
célibataire (définitif)	single; never married
célibataire du sexe féminin	spinster
célibataire du sexe masculin	bachelor
charge, enfants à	dependent children
charge, personne à	dependent, n.
chef du ménage	head of a household

French	English
chiffrer	code, v.
chômeur	unemployed, n.
citoyen	citizen, m.
citoyenneté	nationality
classe	group
classe sociale	social class
classer	classify
cohorte	cohort
cohorte, fécondité d'une	cohort fertility
cohorte fictive	synthetic cohort
coït	coitus
coït interrompu	coitus interruptus
comparatif	standardized (of a rate), m.
composition par âge	age distribution
comptage	count, n.
conception	conception
condom	condom
confession	religion
conjoint	spouse, m.
conjointe	spouse, f.
continence périodique (méthode de)	rhythm method
contraceptif (matériel)	contraceptive, n.
contraceptif oral	oral contraceptive
contraception	contraception
contraception postcoïtale	postcoital contraceptive
contraceptive, méthode	contraceptive method
contrainte morale	moral restraint
contrôle des naissances	birth control
conurbation	conurbation; standard metropolitan area
corrigé	corrected, m.; revised, m.
couleur	color
couple marié	(married) couple
culte	(religious) denomination
cycle menstruel	menstrual cycle

French	English
décès	death
décès, bulletin de	death certificate
décès, cause de	cause of death
décroissement de la population	population decline; negative growth
défaut de réponse	nonresponse
déficience	disability; infirmity
démographe	demographer
démographie	demography
dénombrement	census
densité de la population	population density
départ	departure (of emigrants)
dépendance, rapport de	dependency ratio
dépendant	dependent, n., m.
dépeuplement	depopulation
déplacée, personne	displaced person
dépopulation	depopulation
dépouillement, secteur de	census tract
descendance complète	completed fertility
descendance finale	completed fertility
développement économique (rythme de)	economic development
diagramme	diagram
diaphragme (vaginal)	diaphragm; pessary
dimension de la famille	family size
dispersion	dispersion; scatter
dispositif intra-utérin	intra-uterine device
distribution	(frequency) distribution
district de recensement	census tract
DIU	IUD
division territoriale	territorial unit
divorce	divorce
domicile, personne sans	vagrant; person of no fixed abode
données brutes	basic, crude, primary, raw data
données de base	basic, crude, primary, raw data
données numériques	data

French	English
durée de la vie	longevity; length of life
durée moyenne d'une génération	length of a generation
écart	difference
écart absolu moyen	mean deviation
écart-type	standard deviation
échantillon	sample, n.
échantillon probabiliste	probability sample
échantillon représentatif	representative sample
d'échantillonnage, erreur	sampling error
échelonnement (des naissances)	spacing (of births), n.
écologie humaine	human ecology
effectif moyen de la population	mean population
élément familial principal	nuclear family
émigration	emigration
emploi, ayant un	employed, adj.
emploi, sans	unemployed, adj.
endogène (décès ou mortalité)	endogenous (of a death)
enfant en bas âge	infant
enfants à charge	dependent children
enfants-femmes, rapport	child-woman ratio
enquête	survey, n.
enquête par sondage	sample survey
enquêteur	(survey) interviewer, m.
enrégistrement	registration
enseignement	education
enseignement du premier degré	primary education
enseignement du second degré	secondary education
enseignement primaire	primary education
enseignement secondaire	secondary education
enseignement supérieur	higher education
ensemble	set, n.
énumération	enumeration
épidémique, maladie	epidemic, n.
éponge vaginale	(contraceptive) sponge

French	English
épouse	spouse, f.
époux	spouse, m.
erreur d'échantillonnage	sampling error
erreur-type	standard error
espacement (des naissances)	spacing (of births), n.
espérance de vie	life expectancy; expectation of life
espérance de vie à la naissance	life expectancy at birth
estimation	estimate, n.; estimation
estimer	estimate, v.
état	state, n.
l'état civil, statistiques de	vital statistics
état matrimonial	marital status; civil status; conjugal status
étendue	range, n.; period of a projection
ethnique, groupe	ethnic group
étranger	alien, n., m.
l'étranger, né à	foreign-born, m.
eugénique	eugenics
eugénisme	eugenics
exogène (décès ou mortalité)	exogenous (of a death)
extrapolation	extrapolation
famille	family
famille biologique	nuclear family
famille conjugale	nuclear family
famille, dimension de la	family size
famille nucléaire	nuclear family
famille, planification de la	family planning
famille restreinte	nuclear family
fausse couche	miscarriage
fécondabilité	fecundability
fécondation	fertilization
fécondité	fertility
fécondité d'une cohorte	cohort fertility
fécondité, indice synthétique de	total fertility rate
fécondité, taux de	fertility rate

French	English
féminin, célibataire du sexe	spinster
féminin, individu du sexe	female, n.
femme	woman
femme mariée	married woman
fertilité	fecundity
fétus	fetus
feu	hearth; household
feuille	schedule of a census
fiche	register
fichier de population	population register
fluctuation	fluctuation
fœtus	fetus
fratrie	siblings
génération	generation; cohort
génération, durée moyenne d'une	length of a generation
génération fictive	synthetic cohort
génération hypothétique	synthetic cohort
génération, taux de	age-specific cohort rate
génétique	genetics
gériatrie	geriatrics
gérontologie	gerontology
gestation	gestation
graphique	graph
grappes, sondage en	cluster sampling
gravidité	pregnancy; gestation
grossesse	pregnancy
groupe d'âges	age group
groupe ethnique	ethnic group
groupe social	socio-economic group
groupe socio-économique	socio-economic group
habitant	inhabitant
hameau	hamlet
hérédité	heredity
homme	man

French	English
homme marié	married man
illégitime	illegitimate
illégitimité	illegitimacy
îlot	block, n.
immigration	immigration
imprimé	form, n.
incapacité	disability
indéterminé	not stated; unknown
indice	index; indicator
indice synthétique de fécondité	total fertility rate
individu	individual
individu du sexe féminin	female, n.
individu du sexe masculin	male, n.
infertilité	infecundity; sterility
intensité du peuplement	population density
interpolation	interpolation
interruption (volontaire) de grossesse	induced abortion
intervalle génésique	birth interval
intra-utérin, dispositif	intra-uterine device
jeunes gens	adolescents
lacune d'enrégistrement	(instance of) underregistration
lacune d'énumération	(instance of) underenumeration
langue maternelle	native language; mother tongue
légitime	legitimate
légitimité	legitimacy
lendemain, pilule du	morning-after pill
lien	relationship (to head of household)
limitation des naissances	birth control
lissage	smoothing (of a curve)
localisation du peuplement	geographic distribution of population
locataire	tenant
locataire d'une chambre meublée	lodger
logement	dwelling unit; residence
longévité	(maximum) life span

French	English
machine électronique	(electronic) computer
(machine) perforatrice	punch, n.
(machine) trieuse	sorter (machine)
mal défini	not stated; unknown
mal désigné	not stated; unknown
malades, proportion des	prevalence rate
maladie	disease
maladie épidémique	epidemic, n.
mariage	marriage
mariage consensuel	concubinage
mariage coutumier	consensual union
mariage, durée du	duration of marriage
marié, couple	(married) couple
marié, homme	married man
mariée, femme	married woman
masculin, célibataire du sexe	bachelor
masculin, individu du sexe	male, n.
masculinité, rapport de	sex ratio
maternité	motherhood
matrimonial, état	marital status; civil status; conjugal status
matrimoniale, situation	marital status; civil status; conjugal status
médian	median, adj., m.
médiane	median, n.
membre du ménage	member of a household
ménage	household
ménage, chef du	head of a household
ménage, membre du	member of a household
ménopause	menopause; climacteric
menstruation	menstruation
menstruel, cycle	menstrual cycle
méthode anticonceptionnelle	contraceptive method
méthode contraceptive	contraceptive method
méthode de retrait	withdrawal
migrant	migrant, m.

French	English
migration	migration
migration alternante	commuting, n.
migration de retour	return migration; remigration
migration forcée	forced migration
migration intérieure	internal migration
migration internationale	international migration
migration interne	internal migration
migration nette	net migration
migratoire, balance	net migration
migratoire, mouvement	migration
migratoire, solde	net migration
minimum physiologique	subsistence level
minorité	minority
mobilité	geographical mobility
mobilité sociale	social mobility
mobilité spatiale	spatial mobility
modal	modal, m.
mode	mode
modèle	model, n.
morbidité	morbidity
morbidité (incidente), taux de	incidence rate (of morbidity)
mort	death
mortalité	mortality
mortalité détaillée, table de	complete life table
mortalité différentielle	differential mortality
mortalité fétale	fetal mortality
mortalité infantile	infant mortality
mortalité intra-utérine	fetal mortality
mortalité liée à la maternité	maternal mortality; puerperal mortality
mortalité maternelle	maternal mortality; puerperal mortality
mortalité néonatale	neonatal mortality
mortalité par cause(s), taux de	cause-specific mortality rate
mortalité périnatale	perinatal mortality
mortalité post(-néo)natale	post-neonatal mortality

French	English
mortalité, quotient de	probability of death
mortalité, table abrégée de	abridged life table
mortalité, table complète de	complete life table
mortalité, table de	life table
mortalité, taux de	death rate
mortinaissance	stillbirth
mortinatalité	stillbirth
mouvement général	trend
mouvement migratoire	migration
mouvement particulier	fluctuation
moyen	mean, adj., m.; average, adj., m.
moyen, écart absolu	mean deviation
moyenne	mean, n.
moyenne arithmétique	(arithmetic) mean
moyenne géométrique	geometric mean
moyenne pondérée	weighted mean; weighted average
naissance	birth
naissance, rang de	birth order; parity
naissance vivante	live birth
naissances, contrôle des	birth control
naissances, limitation des	birth control
naissances, planification des	family planning
naissances, prévention des	birth control
naissances, restriction des	birth control
natalité	natality
natalité, taux de	birth rate; fertility rate
nation	nation; people
nationalité	nationality
nationalité d'origine	national origin
naturalisation	naturalization
navette	commuting, n.
navetteur	commuter, m.
né à l'étranger	foreign-born, m.
né dans le pays	native-born, m.

French	English
net	net, m.
niveau de signification	level of significance
niveau de vie	level of living; standard of living
nomade	nomad
nombre (absolu)	number, n.; figure, n.
nombre rond	round number
nombres ronds, attraction des	heaping; bunching
non-célibataire	ever married, adj.
non-déclaré	not stated, m.; unknown, m.
non-réponse	nonresponse
non-spécifié	not stated, m.; unknown, m.
noyau urbain	central city
nuptialité	nuptiality
nuptialité, taux de	marriage rate
obstacle préventif	preventive check
obstacle répressif	positive check
occupant sans titre	squatter
optimum de peuplement	optimum population; population optimum
ovulation	ovulation
ovule	ovum
parents	parents; relative; kin
parité	parity; birth order
passage, personne de	transient, n.
paternité	parenthood; fatherhood
pays	country
pays insuffisament développé	underdeveloped country
pays, né dans le	native-born, m.
pays sous-développé	less developed country; underdeveloped country
pensionnaire	boarder
perforatrice	punch, n.
personne	person
personne à charge	dependent, n.
personne de passage	transient, n.

French	English
personne déplacée	displaced person
personne sans domicile	vagrant; person of no fixed abode
personne sans résidence fixe	vagrant; person of no fixed abode
perspective de population	population forecast
perspective démographique	population forecast
pessaire occlusif	diaphragm; pessary
peuplement	population
peuplement, intensité du	population density
peuplement, localisation du	geographical distribution; spatial distribution
peuplement, optimum de	population optimum; optimum population
pilule (contraceptive)	(contraceptive) pill
pilule du lendemain	morning-after pill
planification de la famille	family planning
planification des naissances	family planning
poid	(statistical) weight
politique de population	population policy
politique démographique	population policy
population	population
population, accroissement de la	population growth
population active	economically active population
population (active) agricole	agricultural population; farm population
population de droit	de jure population; resident population
population de facto	de facto population; enumerated population
population de fait	de facto population; enumerated population
population de jure	de jure population; resident population
population de résidence habituelle	de jure population; resident population
population, décroissement de la	population decline
population, densité de la	population density
population, effectif moyen de la	mean population
population fermée	closed population
population, fichier de	population register
population moyenne	mean population
population optimale	optimum population
population ouverte	open population

French	English
population, perspective de	population forecast
population, politique de	population policy
population présente	de facto population; enumerated population
population, projection de	population projection
population quasi stable	quasi-stable population
population, registre de	population register
population résidante	de jure population; resident population
population stable	stable population
population stationnaire	stationary population
population type	standard population
population type, méthode de la	direct method of standardization
population vivant de l'agriculture	farm population
pourcentage	percentage; percent
précision	accuracy
prématurité	prematurity (of births)
préservatif féminin	diaphragm; pessary
préservatif (masculin)	condom
pression démographique	population pressure
prévention des naissances	birth control
prévision démographique	population forecast
probabilité	probability
probabilité de survie	probability of survival
procréation	reproduction
productivité	productivty
profession	occupation
progéniture	offspring; progeny
projection de la population	population projection
promotion	cohort
proportion	proportion
proportion des malades	prevalence rate
propriétaire	owner; landlord
provisoire	provisional
puberté	puberty
pyramide des âges	population pyramid

French	English
questionnaire	questionnaire
quotient	probability
quotient de mortalité	probability of death
race	race, n.
racine	radix (of a life table)
rajeunissement (démographique)	younging (of a population)
rang d'accouchement	birth order; parity
rang de naissance	birth order; parity
rappel	follow-up, n.
rapport	ratio
rapport de dépendance	dependency ratio
rapport de masculinité	sex ratio
rapport enfants-femmes	child-woman ratio
rapport sexuel	sexual intercourse
recensé	(census) respondent, m.
recensement	census
recensement, district de	census tract
recenseur	enumerator, m.
rectifié	corrected, m.; revised, m.
réfugié	refugee, m.
région	region; territory; area
région naturelle	natural area
registre de population	population register
règle, première	menarche
régulation des naissances	family planning
relation	relationship (to head of household)
religion	religion
remariage	remarriage
renseignements numériques	data
répartition géographique spatiale	geographical distribution
répartition géographique territoriale	geographical distribution
réponse, défaut de	nonresponse
reproduction, taux brut de	gross reproduction rate
reproduction, taux net de	net reproduction rate

French	English
résidence fixe, personne sans	vagrant; person of no fixed abode
restriction des naissances	birth control
résultat élaboré	refined figure
retrait, méthode de	withdrawal
révisé	revised, m.; corrected, m.
révolution démographique	demographic transition
révolution vitale	demographic transition
risque	risk
rural	rural, m.
sans emploi	unemployed, adj.
santé publique	public health
secteur d'activité économique	sector of the economy; industry
secteur de dépouillement	census tract
ségrégation	segregation
sénilité	senility
série	series
série chronologique	time series
seuil de signification	level of significance
sexe	sex
sexe et par groupe d'âges, taux par	sex-age-specific rate
sexe féminin, individu du	female, n.
sexe masculin, individu du	male, n.
signification, niveau de	level of significance
signification, seuil de	level of significance
simulation	simulation
situation matrimoniale	marital status; civil status; conjugal status
solde migratoire	net migration
sondage	sampling, n.
sondage aréolaire	area sampling
sondage en grappes	cluster sampling
sondage, enquête par	sample survey
sondage stratifié	stratified sampling
sortie	departure (of emigrants)
sous-échantillon	subsample

French	English
sous-peuplement	underpopulation
sous-population	subpopulation; underpopulation
spermatozoïde	sperm
statistique de l'état civil	vital statistics
statistiques démographiques	population statistics
stérilet	intra-uterine device
stérilisation	sterilization
stérilisation tubaire	tubal ligation
sterilité	sterility
stratification sociale	social stratification
structure par âge	age structure; age distribution
sujet	subject, n.
surpeuplement	overpopulation
surpopulation	overpopulation
survie, probabilité de	probability of survival
survivant	survivor, m.
table	table, n.
table abrégée de mort	abridged life table
table abrégée de mortalité	abridged life table
table de mortalité	life table; mortality table
table de mortalité détaillée	complete life table
tableau à multiple entrée	cross-tabulation
tableaux, mettre en	tabulate
taux	rate
taux de génération	age-specific rate
taux intrinsèque	intrinsic rate; true rate
taux types, méthode des	indirect method of standardization
tendance générale	trend
territoire	area; territory; region
transition démographique	demographic transition
trieuse	sorter (machine)
tubectomie	salpingectomy
union	union
union consensuelle	consensual union

French	English
union illégitime	free union; concubinage
union légitime	marriage
union libre	consensual union
urbain	urban, m.
urbain, noyau	central city
urbanisation	urbanization
utérus	uterus
variabilité	variation; variability
variable	variable, n.
variation	fluctuation
vasectomie	vasectomy
ventiler	classify
veuf	widower
veuve	widow
viable	viable (of a fetus)
vie, durée de la	longevity; length of life
vie, espérance de	life expectancy; expectation of life
vie, espérance de, à la naissance	life expectancy at birth
vie médiane	median length of life
vie moyenne	mean length of life
vie, niveau de	level of living; standard of living
vie probable	probable length of life
vieillesse	old age
vieillissement (démographique)	aging (of a population)
village	village
ville	city; town

Spanish to English

Spanish	English
aborto	abortion
aborto espontáneo	spontaneous abortion
aborto provocado	induced abortion
abstinencia periódica	periodic abstinence
acta de defunción	death certificate
actividad económica, rama de	sector of the economy; industry
adaptación cultural	acculturation
adolescencia	adolescence
adolescente	adolescent
adulto	adult, n., m.
agente censal	enumerator
aglomeración multimunicipal	standard metropolitan area
agricola, población	farm population; agricultural population
agropecuaria, población	agricultural population; farm population
agrupación urbana	standard metropolitan area
agrupamiento	group
alcance	range
aldea	village
alfabeto	literate person, m.
alma	soul; individual
alumbramiento múltiple	multiple birth
alumbramiento prematuro	premature birth
amplitud	range
análisis	analysis
años vividos, total de	total years lived
anticoncepción	contraception
anticonceptiva, pildora	contraceptive pill
anticonceptivo	contraceptive, n.
anticonceptivo, método	contraceptive method
anticonceptivo oral	oral contraceptive
anticonceptivo post coito	postcoital contraceptive
área metropolitana	standard metropolitan area
área	area; territory; region
área natural	natural area

Spanish	English
áreas, mustreo por	area sampling
arrendatario	tenant, m.
asimilación	assimilation
atracción a ciertos números	heaping; bunching
atributo	attribute; characteristic
autoenumeración	self-enumeration
autoinscripción	self-enumeration
base	base, n.; radix (of a life table)
boletín	schedule, n.
bruta	crude (of a rate)
bruto	gross
cabeza de familia	head of a household
calcular	estimate, v.
campo de variación	range
capital	capital (city)
característica	characteristic; attribute
casada, mujer	married woman
casado, hombre	married man
casamiento	marriage
caserio	hamlet
categoría social	socio-economic group
celibato	celibacy
célibe	single
censado	(census) respondent, m.
censal, agente	enumerator
censo	census
certificado de defunción	death certificate
cifra	number, n.
cifra calculada	refined figure
ciudad	city; town
ciudadano	citizen, m.
civil, estado	marital status
clase	group
clase social	social class

Spanish	English
clasificadora, máquina	sorter (machine)
clasificar	classify
cociente	rate
codificar	code, v.
coeficiente de ponderación	weight (statistical)
cohorte	cohort
cohorte hipotética	synthetic cohort
coito	coitus
coito interrumpido	coitus interruptus
color	color
comparativa	standardized (of a rate), f.
composición por edad	age structure; age distribution
computadora electrónica	(electronic) computer
concepción	conception
concubinato	concubinage
condón	condom
conglomerados, muestreo por	cluster sampling
conjunto	set, n.
conmutante, trabajador*	commuter
control de la natalidad	birth control
control de los nacimientos	birth control
control positivo	positive check
control preventivo	preventive check
cónyuga	spouse, f.
cónyugo	spouse, m.
corregido	corrected
crecimiento de la población	population growth
crecimiento económico	economic growth
crecimiento fisiológico	natural increase
crecimiento natural	natural increase
crecimiento negativo	negative growth
crecimiento vegetativo	natural increase
criatura	infant

*Translates the English, but not a usual term.

Spanish	English
cruda	crude (of a rate)
cuadro	table, n.
cuestionario	questionnaire
culto	(religious) denomination
datos	data
datos básicos	basic, primary, raw data
datos brutos	crude, raw data
datos crudos	crude data
datos primarios	primary, basic data
defunción	death
defunción, acta de	death certificate
defunción, certificado de	death certificate
demografía	demography
demógrafo	demographer, m.
densidad de población	population density
dependencia, razón de	dependency ratio
dependiente	dependent, n.
desarrollo económico	economic development
desarrollo, país en	less developed country; underdeveloped country
descenso de población	population decline
desconocido	unknown, m.
desempleado	unemployed, adj. or n., m.
desplazada, persona	displaced person
despoblación	depopulation
desviación	difference
desviación estandar(d)	standard deviation
desviación media	mean deviation
diafragma	diaphragm
diagrama	diagram
diferencia	difference
dispersión	dispersion; scatter, n.
dispositivo intra-uterino	intra-uterine device
distribución	(frequency) distribution
distribución espacial	geographical distribution; spatial distribution

Spanish	English
distribución geográfica	geographical distribution; spatial distribution
distribución por edad	age distribution; age composition
distribución territorial	geographical distribution; spatial distribution
DIU	IUD
divorcio	divorce
domicilio, persona sin	vagrant; person of no fixed abode
duración de la vida	length of life
duración del matrimonio	duration of marriage
duración media de una generación	length of a generation
ecología humana	human ecology
edad	age
edad, composición por	age structure; age distribution
edad, distribución por	age distribution; age structure
edades, estructura por	age structure; age distribution
edades, grupo de	age group(ing)
edades, intervalo de	age group
edades mas jovenes, con estructura de	younging (of a population)
edades, pirámide de	population pyramid
edades, tasa por	age-specific rate
embarazo	pregnancy
emigración	emigration
empadronador	enumerator, m.
empadronamiento	census; enumeration
empleado	employed, m.
empleo, sin	unemployed, adj.
encuesta	survey, n.; sampling, n.
encuesta por muestra	sample survey
encuesta por muestreo	sample survey
encuesta por sondeo	sample survey
endógena (causa)	endogenous (of a death), f.
enfermedad	disease
enfermos, proporción de	prevalence rate (of disease)
enseñanza media	secondary education
enseñanza primaria	primary education

Spanish	English
enseñanza secundaria	secondary education
enseñanza superior	higher education
entrada	arrival (of immigrants)
entrevistador	(survey) interviewer, m.
enumeración	enumeration
enumerador	enumerator, m.
envejecimiento	aging
epidemia	epidemic, n.
error "estandar(d)"	standard error
error standard	standard error
error típico	standard error
esperanza de vida	life expectancy
esperanza de vida al nacer	life expectancy at birth
espermatozoide	sperm
esponja vaginal	(contraceptive) sponge
esposa	spouse, f.
esposo	spouse, m.
estadísticas vitales	vital statistics
estadísticas de la población	population statistics
estadísticas demográficas	population statistics
estado	state, n.
estado civil	marital status; civil status; conjugal status
estado matrimonial	marital status; civil status; conjugal status
estandar(d)ización, método directo de	direct method of standardization
estandar(d)ización, método indirecto de	indirect method of standardization
estandar(d)izada	standardized (of a rate), f.
esterilidad	sterility
esterilización	sterilization
estimación	estimate, n.; estimation
estimar	estimate, v.
estratificación social	social stratification
estructura por edad	age structure; age distribution
estudio	analysis; survey, n.

Spanish	English
etario, grupo	age group
étnico, grupo	ethnic group
eugenesia	eugenics
exactitud	accuracy
exógena (causa)	exogenous (of a death), f.
expectativa de vida	expectation of life; life expectancy
extranjero	alien, n., m.
extranjero, nacido en el	foreign-born, m.
extrapolación	extrapolation
fallecimiento	death
falta de respuesta	nonresponse
familia	family
familia, cabeza de	head of a household
familia, dimensión de la	family size
familia, jefe de	head of a household
familia, planificación de la	family planning
familia, tamaño de la	family size
familiar, miembro	member of a household
familiar, núcleo	nuclear family
familiar, planificación	family planning
familiar, subsidio	family allowance; family subsidy
fecundabilidad	fecundability
fecundación	fertilization
fecundidad	fertility
fecundidad completada	completed fertility
fecundidad de una cohorte	cohort fertility
fecundidad final	completed fertility
fecundidad, tasa de	fertility rate
fecundidad, tasa global de	total fertility rate
fecundidad, tasa total de	total fertility rate
fertilidad	fecundity
feto	fetus
ficha perforada	punch card
fluctuación	fluctuation

Spanish	English
formulario	form, n.; schedule, n.
fratria	siblings
freno moral	moral restraint
generación	generation
generación, duración media de una	length of a generation
generación ficticia	synthetic cohort
genética	genetics
geriatría	geriatrics
gerontología	gerontology
gestación	gestation
gráfico	graph
grupo	group
grupo de edades	age group(ing)
grupo etario	age group(ing)
grupo social	socio-economic group
grupo socioeconómico	socio-economic group
habitante	inhabitant
hembra	female, n.; woman
herencia	heredity
hijos	offspring; progeny
hijos dependientes	dependent children
hogar	household
hoja	schedule, n.
hombre	man
huésped	boarder; lodger, m.
ilegitimidad	illegitimacy
ilegítimo	illegitimate
impreso, n.	form, n.
incapacidad	disability
incidencia, tasa da	incidence rate
indicador	indicator
índice	index
individuo	individual
infante	infant

Spanish	English
inmigración	immigraton
inquilino	tenant, m.
inscrito	(census) respondent, m.
interpolación	interpolation
intervalo de edades	age bracket
intervalo genésico	birth interval
intervale intergenésico	spacing (of births), n.
intra-uterino, dispositivo	intra-uterine device; IUD
jefe de familia	head of a household
jovenes, con estructura de edades mas	younging (of a population)
lactación (prolongada)	lactation (prolonged)
lapso de vida	life span
legitimidad	legitimacy
legítimo	legitimate, m.
lengua materna	native language; mother tongue
lengua nativa	native language; mother tongue
ligación de tubos	tubal ligation
localidad	village
longevidad	longevity; length of life
lugar	village
mal definido	not stated; unknown
mal especificado	not stated; unknown
malparto	miscarriage
manzana	block, n.
máquina clasificadora	sorter (machine)
máquina perforadora	punch, n.
masculinidad, relación de	sex ratio
maternidad	motherhood
matrimonial, estado	marital status
matrimonial, situación	marital status
matrimonio	marriage
matrimonio, duración del	duration of marriage
matrimonio sucesivo	remarriage
media	mean, n.; average

Spanish	English
media aritmética	mean, n.; average
media geométrica	geometric mean
media ponderada	weighted mean
mediana	median, n.
mediano	median, adj. m.
medio	mean, adj. m.; average, adj. m.
menopausia	menopause
menstruación	menstruation
menstruación, primera	menarche
menstrual, ciclo	menstrual cycle
método anticonceptivo	contraceptive method
método del ritmo	rhythm method; periodic abstinence
migración	migration
migración de retorno	return migration
migración forzosa	forced migration
migración interna	internal migration
migración internacional	international migration
migración neta	net migration
migrante	migrant
migratorio, saldo	net migration
mínimo vital	subsistence level
minoría	minority
moda	mode
modal	modal
modelo	model, n.
morbilidad	morbidity
morbilidad, tasa de	incidence rate
mortalidad	mortality
mortalidad diferencial	differential mortality
mortalidad detallada, tabla de	complete life table
mortalidad fetal	fetal mortality
mortalidad infantil	infant mortality
mortalidad maternal	maternal mortality

135

Spanish	English
mortalidad neonatal	neonatal mortality
mortalidad perinatal	perinatal mortality
mortalidad por causa(s), tasa específica de	cause-specific mortality rate
mortalidad postneonatal	post-neonatal mortality
mortalidad precoz	neonatal mortality
mortalidad puerperal	puerperal mortality
mortalidad, tabla abreviada de	abridged life table
mortalidad, tabla completa de	complete life table
mortalidad, tabla de	life table
mortalidad, tasa de	death rate
mortinatalidad	stillbirth
mortineonatalidad	neonatal mortality
movilidad espacial	geographical mobility
movilidad geográfica	geographical mobility
movilidad social	social mobility
muerte	death
muerte, causa de	cause of death
muerte, probabilidad de	probability of death
muestra	sample, n.
muestra al azar	probability sample
muestra aleatoria	probability sample
muestra, encuesta por	sample survey
muestra estratificada	stratified sample
muestra representativa	representative sample
muestreo	sampling, n.
muestreo, encuesta por	sample survey
muestreo, error de	sampling error
muestreo por áreas	area sampling
muestreo por conglomerados	cluster sampling
muestreo por racimos	cluster sampling
mujer	woman
nacido en el extranjero	foreign-born, m.
nacido en el país	native-born, m.
nacido muerto	stillbirth, m.

Spanish	English
nacido vivo	live birth, m.
nacimiento	birth
nacimiento de niño vivo	live birth
nacimiento múltiple	multiple birth
nacimiento, orden de	birth order
nacimiento prematuro	premature birth
nacimientos, control de los	birth control
nacimientos, regulación de los	birth control
nacimientos, restricción de los	birth control
nación	nation; people (nation)
nacionalidad	nationality
nacionalidad de origen	national origin
natalidad	natality
natalidad, control de la	birth control
natalidad, tasa de	birth rate; fertility rate
naturalización	naturalization
neto	net
niño pequeño	infant, m.
niños-mujeres, relación	child-woman ratio
nivel de significación	level of significance
nivel de subsistencia	subsistence level
nivel de vida	level of living; standard of living
no consta	nonresponse; unknown
no soltero	ever married, adj. m.
nómada	nomad
núcleo familiar	nuclear family
núcleo urbano	central city
número (absoluto)	number, n.
número medio de personas	mean population
número redondeado	round number
números, atracción a ciertos	heaping; bunching
nupcialidad	nuptiality
nupcialidad, tasa de	marriage rate
ocupación	occupation

137

Spanish	English
ocupante sin título	squatter
óptimo de población	population optimum
orden de nacimiento	birth order; parity
ovulación	ovulation
óvulo	ovum
padres	parents
país	country
país en desarrollo	less developed country
país subdesarrollado	underdeveloped country
pareja (matrimonial)	(married) couples
parentesco	relationship (to head of household)
paridez	parity; birth order
parientes	relatives; kin
paternidad	parenthood; fatherhood
pensionista	lodger; boarder
pérdido	miscarriage
perforadora, máquina	punch, n.
persona	person
persona desplazada	displaced person
persona sin residencia fija	person of no fixed abode
persona sin domicilio	person of no fixed abode
perspectiva demográfica	population forecast
pildora anticonceptiva	contraceptive pill
pirámide de edades	population pyramid
planificación de la familia	family planning
planificación familiar	family planning
planilla	schedule, n.
población	population
población abierta	open population
población activa	economically active population
población agrícola	farm population
población agropecuaria	agricultural population
población cerrada	closed population
población, crecimiento de la	population growth

Spanish	English
población cuasi estable	quasi-stable population
población de derecho	de jure population; resident population
población de hecho	de facto population; enumerated population
población, descenso de	population decline
población, densidad de	population density
población estable	stable population
población estacionaria	stationary population
población estándar(d)	standard population
población media	mean population
población óptima	optimum population
población, política de la	population policy
población presente	de facto population; enumerated population
población, presión de la	population pressure
población, registro de la	population register
población rejuveneciéndose	younging population
población residente	de jure population; resident population
política de la población	population policy
ponderación, coeficiente de	(statistical) weight
ponderada, media	weighted mean
ponderado, promedio	weighted mean
por ciento	percent
porcentaje	percentage; percent
precisión	accuracy
predicción demográfica	population forecast
prematuridad	prematurity (of births)
preñez	pregnancy
preservativo	condom; sheath
presión de la población	population pressure
presión demográfica	population pressure
prevalencia, tasa de	prevalence rate
previsión demográfica	population forecast
probabilidad	probability; risk
procreación	reproduction
productividad	productivity

Spanish	English
profesión	occupation
prognóstico demográfico	population forecast
promedio	mean, n.; average
promedio geométrico	geometric mean
promedio ponderado	weighted average; weighted mean
promoción	cohort
pronóstico demográfico	population forecast
propietario	owner; landlord, m.
proporción	proportion; ratio
proporción de enfermos	prevalence rate (of disease)
provisional	provisional
proyección de la población	population projection
proyección demográfica	population projection
pubertad	puberty
pueblo	town; people (nation)
racimos, muestreo por	cluster sampling
raíz (de la tabla de mortalidad)	radix (of a life table)
rama de actividad económica	industry; sector of the economy
raza	race, n.
razón	proportion; ratio
razón de dependencia	dependency ratio
recorrido	range
rectificado	corrected, m.
recuento	count, n.; enumeration
refugiado	refugee, m.
región	region; area; territory
registro	registration
registro de la población	population register
regla, primera	menarche
regulación de los nacimientos	birth control
rejuveneciéndose (población)	younging (of a population)
rejuvenecimiento	younging (of a population)
relación	ratio
relación de masculinidad	sex ratio

Spanish	English
relación niños-mujeres	child-woman ratio
relaciones sexuales	sexual relations
religión	religion
reproducción, tasa bruta de	gross reproduction rate
reproducción, tasa neta de	net reproduction rate
residencia	residence; dwelling unit
residencia fija, persona sin	vagrant; person of no fixed abode
respondente	(census) respondent
respuesta, falta de	nonresponse; unknown
restricción de los nacimientos	birth control
revisado	revised, m.
revolución demográfica	demographic transition; demographic revolution
revolución vital	vital revolution; demographic transition
riesgo	risk
ritmo, método del	rhythm method; periodic abstinence
rural	rural
saldo migratorio	net migration
salida	departure (of emigrants)
salpingectomía	salpingectomy
salubrida pública	public health
salud pública	public health
sanidad pública	public health
sector censal	census tract
sector económico	sector of the economy; industry
segregación	segregation
seguimiento	follow-up, n.
senilidad	senility
serie	series
serie cronológica	time series
serie de tiempo	time series
sexo	sex
sexo femenino, individuo del	female, n.
sexo masculino, individuo del	male, n.

Spanish	English
sexo y por grupos de edades, tasa por	sex-age-specific rate
significación, nivel de	level of significance
simulación	simulation
sin empleo	unemployed, adj.
sin información	not stated; unknown
sin respuesta	nonresponse
situación matrimonial	marital status; civil status; conjugal status
sobrepoblación	overpopulation
sobrevisión	survey, n.
sobrevivencia, probabilidad de	probability of survival
sobrevisión muestral	sample survey
social, categoría	socio-economic group
social, grupo	socio-economic group
socioeconómico, grupo	socio-economic group
soltera	spinster; single, f.
soltero	bachelor; single, m.
sondeo	sampling, n.
sondeo, encuesta por	sample survey; sampling, n.
suavizamiento	smoothing (of a curve)
subdesarrollado, país	underdeveloped country; less developed country
subenumeración	underenumeration
submuestra	subsample
subpoblación	subpopulation; underpopulation
subregistro	underregistration
subsidio familiar	family allowance; family subsidy
subsistencia, nivel de	subsistence level
suburbio	suburb
sujeto	subject, n., m.
superficie	area; territory; region
superpoblación	overpopulation
supervivencia, probabilidad de	probability of survival
superviviente	survivor
tabla	table, n.

Spanish	English
tabla abreviada de mortalidad	abridged life table
tabla completa de mortalidad	complete life table
tabla de mortalidad	life table; mortality table
tabla de mortalidad detallada	complete life table
tabla de vida	life table; mortality table
tabulación cruzada	cross-tabulation
tabulación de múltiple entradas	cross-tabulation
tabular	tabulate
tamaño de la familia	family size
tasa	rate
tasa intrinseca	intrinsic rate
tasa real	true rate; intrinsic rate
tendencia	trend
territorio	territory; area; region
total de años vividos	total years lived
trabajador conmutante*	commuter, m.
transeúnte	transient, n.
transición demográfica	demographic transition
tubos, ligación de	tubal ligation
unión	union
unión consensual	consensual union
unión ilegítima	free union
unión libre	consensual union
urbanización	urbanization
urbano	urban, m.
útero	uterus
vagabundo	vagrant; person of no fixed abode, m.
valor central	median, n.
valor dominante	mode
valor estimado	estimate, n.
variabilidad	variability
variable	variable, n.
variación	dispersion; fluctuation; scatter, n.; variation

*Translates the English, but not a usual term.

Spanish	English
variación, campo de	range
varón	male, n.
vasectomía	vasectomy
vejez	old age
viable	viable (of a fetus)
vida, duración de la	length of life
vida, esperanza de	life expectancy
vida, esperanza de, al nacer	expectation of life at birth
vida, expectativa de	life expectancy
vida, lapso de	life span
vida media	mean length of life
vida mediana	median length of life
vida, nivel de	level of living; standard of living
vida probable	probable length of life
vida, tabla de	life table; mortality table
villa	town; village
visitador	(survey) interviewer, m.
vivienda	dwelling unit
zona	area; territory; region

Italian–English

Italian	English
abitante	inhabitant
abitazione	dwelling unit
aborto	abortion
aborto involontario	spontaneous abortion
aborto procurato	induced abortion
aborto provocato	induced abortion
aborto spontaneo	spontaneous abortion
accrescimento naturale	natural increase
accuratezza	accuracy
acquisto della cittadinanza	naturalization
adattamento culturale	acculturation
adolescente	adolescent, n.
adolescenza	adolescence
adulto	adult, n., m.
affini	relatives; kin
agente di censimento	enumerator
agglomerato (multicomunale)	standard metropolitan area
agglomerazione (multicomunale) metropolitana	standard metropolitan area
agricoltura, popolazione vivente di	agricultural population; farm population
alfabeta	literate person
allattamento (prolungato)	(prolonged) lactation
analisi	analysis
andamento particolare	fluctuation
andare e venire	commuting, n.
anima	soul; individual
anni vissuti, numero totale di	total years lived
anticoncezionale	contraceptive, n.
anticoncezionale, metodo	contraceptive method
anticoncezionale, pratica	contraceptive method
area	area
area metropolitana	standard metropolitan area
aree, sondaggio per	area sampling
arrivo	arrival (of immigrants)
all'arrotondamento, tendenza	heaping; bunching

Italian	English
assegno familiare	family allowance
assimilazione	assimilation
attività economica, ramo di	industry; sector of the economy
attività economica, settore di	industry; sector of the economy
attività individuale	occupation
attrazione dei numeri arrotondati	heaping; bunching
autoenumerazione	self-enumeration
bambini-donne, rapporto	child-woman ratio
borgata	village
borgo	hamlet; village
base	base, n.
calcolatore elettronico	(electronic) computer
calcolo	count, n.
campionamento a grappolo	cluster sampling
campionamento, errore di	sampling error
campionamento stratificato	stratified sampling
campione	sample, n.
campione probabilistico	probability sample
campione rappresentativo	representative sample
campo di variazione	range
capitale	capital (city)
capofamiglia	head of a household
carattere mutabile	characteristic; attribute
carattere qualitativo	characteristic; attribute
carico, figli a	dependent children
carico, persona a	dependent, n.
caseggiato	block, n.
caso	chance; risk
categoria socio-economica	socio-economic group
causa di morte	cause of death
celibato	celibacy (of males)
celibe	bachelor; single
celibe e nubile	never married
censimento	census

Italian	English
censimento, agente di	enumerator
censimento, sezione di	census tract
censimento, ufficiale di	enumerator
censito	(census) respondent, m.
centro urbano	central city
certificato di morte	death certificate
ciclo mestruale	menstrual cycle
cifra	figure, n.; number, n.
cifra rotonda	round number
cifra tonda	round number
circolazione sociale	social mobility
circoscrizione comunale	census tract
città	city
cittadinanza	nationality
cittadinanza, acquisto della	naturalization
cittadino	citizen, m.
classe	group
classe pluriennale d'età	age group
classe poliennale d'età	age group
classe sociale	social class
classificare	classify
classificatore	(machine) sorter
coabitazione	cohabitation
codificare	code, v.
coefficiente di ponderazione	(statistical) weight
coefficienti tipi, metodo dei	indirect method of standardization
coito	coitus
coito interrotto	coitus interruptus; withdrawal
colore	color
comparativo (tasso)	standardized (of a rate)
composizione per età	age structure; age distribution
concepimento	conception
concubinato	concubinage
congiunti	relatives; kin

Italian	English
coniugata, (persona) comunque	ever married
continenza periodica, metodo della	periodic abstinence; rhythm method
contracettività	contraception
contracettivo orale	oral contraceptive
contracettivo postcoitale	postcoital contraceptive; morning-after pill
contracettivo successivo al coito	postcoital contraceptive; morning-after pill
contracettivo successivo al rapporto	postcoital contraceptive; morning-after pill
controllo delle nascite	birth control
controllo delle nascite, metodo di	contraceptive method
conurbazione	conurbation
coorte	cohort
coorte, fecondità di una	cohort fertility
coorte fittizia	synthetic cohort
coorte sintetica	synthetic cohort
coppia maritata	(married) couple
correzione indiretta, metodo della	indirect method of standardization
crescita della popolazione	population growth
crescita economica	economic growth; economic development
crescita negativa	negative growth
culto	(religious) denomination
dati	data
dati fondamentali	basic data
dati grezzi	crude data
dati primarii	raw data
dato elaborato*	refined figure
decesso	death
declino della popolazione	population decline; negative growth
declino demografico	depopulation
demografia	demography
demografo	demographer, m.
densità della popolazione	population density
depurato	revised, m.

*Gives the sense of the English phrase but is seldom used.

149

Italian	English
deviazione dalla media	mean deviation
diaframma	diaphragm; pessary
diagramma	diagram
differenza	difference
dimensionamento della famiglia	family planning
dimensione della famiglia	family size
dimora	residence
dimora, persona senza fissa	vagrant, n.
dipendenza, indice di	dependency ratio
disoccupato	unemployed, adj., n., m.
dispersione	dispersion; scatter
distribuzione	(frequency) distribution
distribuzione geografica	geographic distribution; spatial distribution
distribuzione per età	age distribution
distribuzione spaziale	spatial distribution; geographic distribution
distribuzione territoriale	geographic distribution; spatial distribution
discendenza	offspring; progeny
divorzio	divorce
donna	woman
donna coniugata	married woman
donna sposata	married woman
dozzinante	lodger
durata del matrimonio	duration of marriage
durata della vita	length of life
durata media di una generazione	length of a generation
durata media di vita	mean length of life
ecologia umana	human ecology
elenco	schedule, n.
emigrazione	emigration
endogena (causa)	endogenous (of a death)
entrata	arrival (of immigrants)
enumeratore	enumerator
enumerazione	enumeration
epidemia	epidemic, n.

Italian	English
eredità	heredity
ereditarietà	heredity
errore	error; difference
errore di campionamento	sampling error
errore medio	standard error
errore quadratico medio	standard error
esogena (causa)	exogenous (of a death)
espatrio	departure (of emigrants)
all'estero, nato	foreign-born, m.
estrapolazione	extrapolation
età	age
d'età, classe pluriennale	age bracket; age group(ing)
d'età, classe poliennale	age bracket; age group(ing)
età, composizione per	age distribution; age structure
età, distribuzione per	age distribution; age structure
l'età, gruppo secondo	age group(ing); age bracket
età, piramide delle	population pyramid
età, quoziente specifico per	age-specific rate
età senile	old age
età, struttura per	age structure; age distribution
l'età, tasso secondo	age-specific rate
eugenica	eugenics
extrapolazione	extrapolation
famiglia	family
famiglia (in senso statistico)	household
famiglia, dimensionamento della	family planning
famiglia, dimensione della	family size
famiglia, grandezza della	family size
famiglia nucleare	nuclear family
famiglia, pianificazione della	family planning
fecondabilità	fecundability
fecondazione	fertilization
fecondità	fertility
fecondità complessiva	completed fertility

151

Italian	English
fecondità di una coorte	cohort fertility
fecondità di una generazione	cohort fertility
fecondità finale	completed fertility
fecondità finale, indice cumulativo di	total fertility rate
fecondità, quoziente di	fertility rate
fecondità, tasso di	fertility rate
fecondità, tasso totale di	total fertility rate
fecondità totale	completed fertility
femmina	female, n.; woman
fertilità	fecundity
feto	fetus
figli	offspring; progeny
figli a carico	dependent children
figli e donne, rapporto fra	child-woman ratio
figliolanza	offspring; progeny
fluttuazione	fluctuation
foglio	schedule, n.
forestiero	alien, n., m.
fratellanza	siblings
frazione della popolazione	subpopulation
freno morale	preventive check; moral restraint
freno preventivo	preventive check
freno repressivo	positive check
generazione	generation; cohort
generazione, durata media di una	length of a generation
generazione, fecondità di una	cohort fertility
generazione fittizia	synthetic cohort
generazione ipotetica	synthetic cohort
generazioni successive, intervallo medio fra	length of a generation
genetica	genetics
geriatria	geriatrics
genitori	parents
gerontologia	gerontology
gestazione	gestation

Italian	English
graduazione	smoothing (of a curve)
grafico	graph
grandezza della famiglia	family size
grappolo, sondaggio a	cluster sampling
gravidanza	pregnancy
gravidanza, interruzione della	abortion
greggio	crude (of a rate), m.
grezzo	crude (of a rate), m.
gruppo	group
gruppo etnico	ethnic group
gruppo secondo l'età	age group(ing)
gruppo socio-economico	socio-economic group
ignoto	unknown, m.
illegittimità	illegitimacy
illegittimo	illegitimate, m.
immigrazione	immigration
inabilità	disability
inchiesta	survey, n.
inchiesta campionaria	sample survey
inchiesta por sondaggio	sample survey
incidenza, tasso di	incidence rate
incremento della popolazione	population growth
incremento naturale	natural increase
incremento negativo	negative growth
indagine	survey, n.
indagine campionario	sample survey
indicatore	indicator
indice	index
indice cumulativo di fecondità finale	total fertility rate
indice di dipendenza	dependency ratio
indice di nuzialità	marriage rate
individuo	individual
infante	infant
infertilità	infecundity

Italian	English
ingresso	arrival (of immigrants)
inquilino	tenant, m.; lodger, m.
insieme	set, n.
intensità del popolamento	population density
interpolazione	interpolation
interruzione della gravidanza	abortion
intervallo	spacing (of births), n.
intervallo genesico	birth interval
intervallo medio fra generazioni successive	length of a generation
intervallo tra nascite	birth interval
intervistato	respondent, m.
intervistatore	interviewer; enumerator
invalidità	disability
invecchiamento	aging, n.
isolamento	segregation
isolato	block, n.
istruzione elementare	primary education
istruzione media	secondary education
istruzione primaria	primary education
istruzione secondaria	secondary education
istruzione superiore	higher education
lacuna nella registrazione	underregistration
legamento delle tube	tubal ligation
legittimità	legitimacy
legittimo	legitimate, m.
limite di sussistenza	subsistence level
lingua materna	mother tongue
lista	schedule, n.
livello di significatività	level of significance
livello di sussistenza	subsistence level
locatario	tenant, m.
locatario di camera ammobiliata	lodger, m.
longevità	longevity; life span
lordo	gross, m.

Italian	English
macchina perforatrice	punch, n.
macchina selezionatrice	(machine) sorter
madre lingua	mother tongue
mal definito	not stated, m.
malati, proporzione di	prevalence rate
malattia	disease
malattia epidemica	epidemic, n.
mancata risposta	nonresponse
maschio	male, n.
mascolinità, rapporto di	sex ratio
maternità	motherhood
maternità, mortalità dovuta alla	maternal mortality; puerperal mortality
matrimonio	marriage
matrimonio, durata del	duration of marriage
matrimonio successivo al primo	remarriage
media	mean, n.
media geometrica	geometric mean
media ponderata	weighted mean
mediana	median, n.
mediano	median, adj., m.
medio	mean, adj., m.
membro della famiglia	member of a household
menarca (pubertà)	menarche
menopausa	menopause
mestruazione	menstruation
metodo anticoncezionale	contraceptive method
metodo dei coefficienti tipo	indirect method of standardization
metodo della continenza periodica	periodic abstinence
metodo della correzione indiretta	indirect method of standardization
metodo della mortalità tipo	indirect method of standardization
metodo della popolazione tipo	direct method of standardization
metodo di controllo delle nascite	contraceptive method
mezzo anticoncezionale	contraceptive, n.
migrante	migrant

155

Italian	English
migrazione	migration
migrazione coatta	forced migration
migrazione con l'estero	international migration
migrazione di ritorno	return migration
migrazione estera	international migration
migrazione forzata	forced migration
migrazione interna	internal migration
migrazione internazionale	international migration
migrazione netta	net migration
minoranza	(ethnic) minority
misura della nuzialità	marriage rate
mobilità geografica	geographic mobility; spatial mobility
mobilità sociale	social mobility
mobilità spaziale	spatial mobility; geographic mobility
mobilità territoriale	geographic mobility; spatial mobility
moda	mode
modale	modal
modello	model, n.; form, n.
modulo	form, n.
morbilità	morbidity
morbosità	morbidity
morbosità, quoziente di	incidence rate
mortalità	mortality
mortalità abbreviata, tavola di	abridged life table
mortalità completa, tavola di	complete life table
mortalità differenziale	differential mortality
mortalità dovuta alla maternità	maternal mortality
mortalità fetale	fetal mortality
mortalità infantile	infant mortality
mortalità intrauterina	fetal mortality
mortalità materna	maternal mortality; puerperal mortality
mortalità neonatale	neonatal mortality
mortalità per causa, quoziente di	cause-specific mortality rate
mortalità per causa, tasso di	cause-specific mortality rate

Italian	English
mortalità perinatale	perinatal mortality
mortalità post-neonatale	post-neonatal mortality
mortalità prenatale	fetal mortality
mortalità puerperale	puerperal mortality
mortalità, quoziente di	death rate
mortalità, tasso di	death rate
mortalità, tavola abbreviata di	abridged life table
mortalità, tavola completa di	complete life table
mortalità, tavola di	life table; mortality table
mortalità tipo, metodo della	indirect method of standardization
morte	death
morte, causa di	cause of death
morte, certificato di	death certificate
morte, probabilità di	probability of death
morte, scheda individuale di	death certificate
movimenti a spola	commuting, n.
nascita	birth
nascita di un nato vivo	live birth, m.
nascita, ordine di	birth order; parity
nascita prematura	premature birth
nascite, controllo delle	birth control
nascite, intervallo tra	birth interval
nascite, planificazione delle	family planning
nascite, regolamentazione delle	birth control
nascite, regolazione della	birth control
natalità	natality
natalità, quoziente di	birth rate
natalità, quoziente generico di	birth rate
natimortalità	stillbirth
nato all'estero	foreign-born, m.
nato nel paese	native-born, m.
nato vivo	live birth, m.
naturalizzazione	naturalization
nazionalità	nationality

Italian	English
nazionalità d'origine	national origin
nazione	nation; people
neonati, vita media dei	life expectancy at birth; mean length of life
neonati, vita probabile dei	median length of life; probable length of life
nessuna risposta	nonresponse
netto	net
nomade	nomad
non analfabeta	literate person
non celibe	ever married, adj.
non indicato	not stated, m.
non specificato	not stated, m.
norma	mode
normalizzato (tasso)	standardized (of a rate)
normalizzazione diretta	direct method of standardization
normalizzazione indiretta	indirect method of standardization
nubilato	celibacy (of females)
nubile	spinster
nucleo familiare principale	nuclear family
nucleo urbano	central city
numeri arrotondati, attrazione dei	heaping; bunching
numero	number, n.
numero totale di anni vissuti	total years lived
nuzialità	nuptiality
nuzialità, indice di	marriage rate
nuzialità, misura della	marriage rate
nuzialità, tasso di	marriage rate
occupante senza titolo	squatter
occupato	employed, m.
occupazione	occupation
optimum di popolazione	population optimum
ordine di nascita	birth order; parity
ostacolo preventivo	preventive check
ostacolo repressivo	positive check
ovulazione	ovulation

158

Italian	English
paese	country; village
paese in via di sviluppo	developing country
paese meno sviluppato	less developed country; underdeveloped country
parenti	relatives; kin
parità	parity; birth order
parto avanti termine	premature birth
parto multiplo	multiple birth
parto plurimo	multiple birth
parto prematuro	premature birth
passaggio, persona di	transient, n.
paternità	parenthood
pensionante	boarder
percentuale	percentage
perequazione	smoothing (of a curve)
perforatrice, macchina	punch. n.
periodo mestruale	menstrual cycle
persona	person
persona a carico	dependent, n.
persona di passaggio	transient, n.
persona senza fissa dimora	vagrant
persona temporaneamente presente	transient, n.
peso	(statistical) weight
pessario	pessary; diaphragm; cervical cap
pianificazione della famiglia	family planning
pianificazione delle nascite	family planning
piccolo villaggio rurale	hamlet
pillola contraccettiva	contraceptive pill
piramide delle età	population pyramid
politica della popolazione	population policy
politica demografica	population policy
ponderazione, coefficiente di	(statistical) weight
popolamento, intensità del	population density
popolazione	population
popolazione agricola	agricultural population; farm population

Italian	English
popolazione aperta	open population
popolazione attiva	economically active population
popolazione censita	de facto population; enumerated population
popolazione chiusa	closed population
popolazione, crescita della	population growth
popolazione de jure	de jure population; resident population
popolazione, densità della	population density
popolazione di diritto	de jure population; resident population
popolazione di fatto	de facto population; enumerated population
popolazione enumerata	de facto population; enumerated population
popolazione, frazione della	subpopulation
popolazione in declino	population decline
popolazione, incremento della	population growth
popolazione legale	de jure population; resident population
popolazione media	mean population
popolazione, optimum di	population optimum; optimum population
popolazione ottima	optimum population; population optimum
popolazione, politica della	population policy
popolazione presente	de facto population; enumerated population
popolazione quasi stabile	quasi-stable population
popolazione, registro della	population register
popolazione residente	de jure population; resident population
popolazione stabile	stable population
popolazione stazionaria	stationary population
popolazione tipo	standard population
popolazione tipo, metodo della	direct method of standardization
popolazione vivente di agricoltura	agricultural population; farm population
pratica anticoncezionale	contraceptive method
precisione	accuracy
preliminario	provisional
prematurità	prematurity (of births)
premio familiare	family allowance; family subsidy
preservativo	condom; sheath
pressione demografica	population pressure

Italian	English
previsione demografica	population forecast
probabilità	probability
probabilità di morte	probability of death
probabilità di sopravvivenza	probability of survival
probabilità di vita	probability of survival
procreazione	reproduction
produttività	productivity
professione	occupation
profilattico	condom; sheath
profugo	refugee, m.
progenie	progeny
programma	schedule, n.
proiezione demografica	population projection
prole	offspring; progeny
proporzione	proportion
proporzione di malati	prevalence rate
proprietario	owner; landlord; m.
prospettiva demografica	population forecast
provvisorio	provisional
pubertà	puberty
questionario	questionnaire
quoziente	rate
radice	radix (of a life table)
ramo di activ ità economica	sector of the economy; industry
rapporto	ratio
rapporto bambini-donne	child-woman ratio
rapporto dei sessi	sex ratio
rapporto di mascolinità	sex ratio
rapporto sessuale	sexual intercourse
rapporto tra figli e donne	child-woman ratio
razza	race, n.
regione	region
regione naturale	natural area
registrazione	registration

Italian	English
registrazione, lacuna nella	underregistration
registro della popolazione	population register
regolamentazione delle nascite	birth control
regolazione delle nascite	birth control
relazione (col capofamiglia)	relationship (to head of household)
religione	religion
residenza	residence
rettificato	corrected, m.
rifugiato	refugee, m.
rilevazione campionaria	sampling, n.
rimpatrio	return migration; remigration
riproduttività	reproduction
riproduttività feminile, saggio lordo di	gross reproduction rate
riproduttività feminile, saggio netto di	net reproduction rate
riproduttività feminile, tasso lordo di	gross reproduction rate
riproduttività feminile, tasso netto di	net reproduction rate
riproduzzione, saggio lordo di	gross reproduction rate
riproduzzione, saggio netto di	net reproduction rate
rischio	risk
ritmo	rhythm method; periodic abstinence
riveduto	revised, m.
rivoluzione demografica	demographic transition
rurale	rural
saggio	rate
saggio intrinseco	intrinsic rate
saggio lordo di riproduttività	gross reproduction rate
saggio lordo di riproduttività feminile	gross reproduction rate
saggio netto di riproduttività	net reproduction rate
saggio netto di reproduttività feminile	net reproduction rate
saggio vero	intrinsic rate
saldo migratorio	net migration
salpingectomia	salpingectomy
sanità pubblica	public health
scarto	difference

Italian	English
scarto semplice medio	mean deviation
scheda	form, n.; schedule, n.
scheda individuale di morte	death certificate
scheda meccanografica	punch card
scheda perforata	punch card
sconosciuto	unknown, m.
scostamento	difference
scostamento quadratico medio	standard deviation
scostamento semplice medio	mean deviation
secondo matrimonio	remarriage (literally, second marriage)
segregazione	segregation
senilità	senility
serie	series
serie cronologica	time series
serie storica	time series
serie temporale	time series
sessi, rapporto dei	sex ratio
sesso	sex
sesso ed età, quoziente specifico per	sex-age-specific rate
sesso ed età, tasso specifico per	sex-age-specific rate
settore di attività economica	sector of the economy; industry
sezione di censimento	census tract
significatività, levello di	level of significance
simulazione	simulation
sobborgo	suburb
soggetto	subject, n., m.
sollecito*	follow-up, n.
sondaggio	sampling, n.
sondaggio a grappolo	cluster sampling
sondaggio campionario	sample survey
sondaggio casuale stratificato	stratified sampling
sondaggio, inchiesta por	sample survey

*Does not translate the English exactly—ordinarily would refer to a second mailing of a postal questionnaire.

163

Italian	English
sondaggio per area	area sampling
sondaggio probabilistico	probability sample
sopravvivente	survivor
sopravvivenza, probabilità di	probability of survival
sottocampione	subsample
sottoenumerazione	underenumeration
sottopopolamento	underpopulation
sottopopolazione	subpopulation; underpopulation
sottoregistrazione	underregistration
sovrapopolamento	overpopulation
sovrapopolazione	overpopulation
spazio	spacing (of births), n.
speranza di vita	life expectancy
speranza di vita alla nascita	life expectancy at birth
spermatozoo	sperm
spirale	intra-uterine device
sposa	spouse; wife
sposo	spouse; husband
sposi	(married) couple
spopolamento	depopulation
spostamenti pendolari	commuting, n.
spugna vaginale	(contraceptive) sponge
squarto quadratico medio	standard deviation
stampato	form, n.
standard di vita	standard of living
standardizzato (tasso)	standardized (of a rate)
standardizzazione diretta	direct method of standardization
standardizzazione indiretta	indirect method of standardization
statistiche dello stato civile	vital statistics
statistiche demografiche	population statistics
stato	state, n.
stato civile	conjugal status; marital status; civil status
stato coniugale	civil status; marital status; conjugal status
stato matrimoniale	marital status; civil status; conjugal status

Italian	English
sterilità	sterility
sterilizzazione	sterilization
stima	estimate, n.
stimare	estimate, v.
straniero	alien, n., m.
stratificazione sociale	social stratification
struttura per età	age structure
subcampione	subsample
subpopolazione	subpopulation
suburbio	suburb
successione	series
suddito	subject, n., m.
sussidio familiare	family subsidy; family allowance
sussistenza, limite di	subsistence level
sussistenza, livello di	subsistence level
sviluppo economico	economic development
sviluppo, paese in via di	less developed country; underdeveloped country
tabella a multiple entrata	cross-tabulation
tabella a plurima entrata	cross-tabulation
tabulare	tabulate
tasso	rate
tasso intrinseco	intrinsic rate
tavola	table, n.
tavola con entrate multiple	cross-tabulation
tavola abbreviata di mortalità	abridged life table
tavola completa di mortalità	complete life table
tavola di mortalità	life table; mortality table
tavola di mortalità abbreviata	abridged life table
tavola di mortalità completa	complete life table
tendenza all'arrotondamento	heaping; bunching
tendenza di fondo	trend
tendenza (generale)	trend
tenore di vita	level of living; standard of living

Italian	English
territorio	territory
tipo, popolazione	standard population
transizione demografica	demographic transition
tube, legamento delle	tubal ligation
ufficiale di censimento	enumerator
unione	union
unione consensuale	consensual union
unione libera	free union
uomo	man
uomo sposato	married man
uovo	ovum
urbanesimo	urbanization
urbanizzazione	urbanization
urbano	urban, m.
uscita	departure (of emigrants)
utero	uterus
valore più frequente	mode
valore stimato	estimate, n.
variabile	variable, n.
variabilità	dispersion; scatter; variation; variability
variazione	variation; variability
variazione, campo di	range
variazione particolare	fluctuation
variazione secolare	trend
vasectomia	vasectomy
vecchiaia	old age
viaggiatore giornaliero	commuter
villaggio	village
visita ripetuta*	follow-up, n.
vita, durata della	length of life; longevity
vita media	life expectancy; expectation of life
vita media alla nascita	life expectancy at birth; mean length of life

*Does not translate the English exactly—ordinarily refers to another house call by a doctor.

Italian	English
vita media dei neonati	mean length of life; life expectancy at birth
vita mediana	median length of life
vita mediana alla nascita	median length of life
vita probabile	probable length of life
vita probabile dei neonati	probable length of life
vita, probabilità di	probability of survival
vita, speranza di	expectation of life; live expectancy
vita, speranza di, alla nascita	life expectancy at birth
vita, standard di	level of living; standard of living
vita, tenore di	level of living; standard of living
vitale	viable (of a fetus)

German to English

German	English
abgeleitete Zahl	refined figure
abhängige Kinder	dependent children
Abnahme der Bevölkerung	population decline
Abort	abortion
Abort, künstlicher	induced abortion
Abortus	abortion
Abwanderung	departure (of emigrants)
Abweichung, durchschnittliche quadratische	standard deviation
Abweichung, mittlere	standard error
Abweichung, mittlere (einfache)	mean deviation
Abweichung, mittlere (quadratische)	standard deviation
Agglomeration, städtische	standard metropolitan area; agglomeration; conurbation
Agglomeration (vielgemeindliche)	standard metropolitan area; agglomeration; conurbation
Alter	age
Alter, fortgeschrittenes	old age
Alter, hohes	old age
Alter, jugendliches	adolescence
alters- und geschlechtsspezifische Rate	age-sex-specific rate
Altersaufbau	age distribution; age structure
Altersgliederung	age distribution; age structure
Altersgruppe	age group(ing)
Altersgruppe, Ziffer nach dem Geschlecht und	sex-age-specific rate
Alterspyramide	population pyramid
Altersschwäche	senility
altersspezifische Rate	age-specific rate
altersspezifische Ziffer	age-specific rate
Altersstruktur	age structure
Altersverteilung	age distribution
Alterung	aging
Analyse	analysis
Aneinanderreihung	series
Angabe, ohne	unknown
Angaben	data

German	English
Angehöriger	dependent, n., m.
Ankunft	arrival (of immigrants)
Anpassung, kulturelle	acculturation
Ansiedler auf fremden Boden	squatter, m.
Anteil	proportion
antikonzeptionelle Methode	contraceptive method
arbeitslos	unemployed, adj.
Arbeitsloser	unemployed, n., m.
Arbeitsunfähigkeit	disability
arithmetisches Mittel	mean, n.; average, n.
arithmetisches Mittel, gewogenes	weighted mean; weighted average
Assimilation	assimilation
Ausgangsdaten	basic data
Ausgangsmasse	radix (of a life table)
Ausgleichung	smoothing (of a curve)
im Ausland geboren	foreign-born, adj.
Ausländer	alien, n., m.
Aussicht	risk
Aussiedler	displaced person, m.; refugee, m.
Auswanderung	emigration; departure (of emigrants)
Auszählung	count, n.
Baby	baby
Basis	base, n.
Basisgrösse	base, n.
Basiszahl	base, n.
bearbeitete Zahl	refined figure
Befrager	interviewer, m.
Befragung	survey, n.
Befruchtung	fertilization
Beischlaf	sexual intercourse
Beischlaf, unterbrochener	coitus interruptus
Belastungsquote (demographische)	dependency ratio
Beobachtungsreihe	set, n.
bereinigt	corrected

German	English
berichtigt	revised
Beruf	occupation
Berufszugehörige der Landwirtschaft	agricultural population; farm population
Beschäftigungsloser	unemployed, n., m.
Besiedlungsdichte	population density
Bevölkerung	population
Bevölkerung, Abnahme der	population decline
Bevölkerung, geschlossene	closed population
Bevölkerung, landwirtschaftliche	agricultural population
Bevölkerung, mittlere	mean population
Bevölkerung, offene	open population
Bevölkerung, optimale	optimum population
Bevölkerung, ortsanwesende	defacto population; enumerated population
Bevölkerung, quasi-stabile	quasi-stable population
Bevölkerung, stabile	stable population
Bevölkerung, stationäre	stationary population
Bevölkerung, Wachstum der	population growth
Bevölkerungsbewegung, Statistik der natürlichen	vital statistics
Bevölkerungsdichte	population density
Bevölkerungsdruck	population pressure
Bevölkerungsgruppe	subpopulation
Bevölkerungslehre	demography
Bevölkerungsoptimum	population optimum
Bevölkerungspolitik	population policy
Bevölkerungsprognose	population forecast
Bevölkerungsrprojektion	population projection
Bevölkerungsregister	population register
Bevölkerungsrückgang	population decline
Bevölkerungsschrumpfung	population decline
Bevölkerungsstatistiken	population statistics
Bevölkerungstrennung	segregation
Bevölkerungsvorausberechnung	population projection
Bevölkerungsvoraussage	population forecast
Bevölkerungswachstum	population growth

172

German	English
Bevölkerungswissenschaft	demography
Bevölkerungswissenschaftler	demographer, m.
Bevölkerungszunahme	population growth
Bevölkerungszuwachs	population growth
Bevölkerungszuwachs, natürlicher	natural increase
Bewohner	inhabitant, m.
Beziehungszahl	ratio
Binnenwanderung	internal migration
Block	block, n.
Blutsverwandte	relatives; kin
Brutto-	gross
Bruttoreproduktionsrate	gross reproduction rate
Bündeln (von Zahlen)	heaping; bunching
Cervix Kappe	cervical cap; diaphragm
Chance	chance; risk
coitus interruptus	coitus interruptus
Daten	data
Daten, rohe	crude data
Demograph	demographer, m.
Demographie	demography
demographische Revolution	demographic revolution; demographic transition
demographische Transformation	demographic transition
demographischer Übergang	demographic transition
Diagram	diagram
dichtester Wert	mode
Differenz	difference
differenzielle Sterblichkeit	differential mortality
Dispersion	dispersion; scatter; variation
Dorf	village
durchlebte Zeit	total years lived
durchlebte Jahre, Gesamtzahl der	total years lived
Durchreisender	transient, n., m.
Durchschnitt	mean, n.; average, n.

German	English
Durchschnitt, gewogener	weighted average; weighted mean
durchschnittliche Lebensdauer	mean length of life; life expectancy at birth
durchschnittliche quadratische Abweichung	standard deviation
Ehe (legale)	marriage
Ehe, freie	free union
Ehe (rechtmässige)	marriage
eheähnliche Gemeinschaft	concubinage
Ehedauer	duration of marriage
Ehegatte	spouse, m.
Ehegattin	spouse, f.
ehelich	legitimate
Ehelichkeit	legitimacy
Ehelosigkeit	celibacy
Ehepaar	(married) couple
Ehescheidung	divorce
Eheschliessungsziffer	marriage rate
Ei	ovum
Eiausstoss	ovulation
Eigenschaft	characteristic; attribute
Eigentümer	owner, m.; landlord, m.
Einbürgerung	naturalization
Eingeborener	native-born, n., m.
Eingliederung	assimilation
Einwanderung	immigration; arrival (of immigrants)
Einwohner	inhabitant, m.
Elementarausbildung	elementary education
Eltern	parents
Elternschaft	parenthood
Empfängnis	conception
Empfängnisfähigkeit	fecundability
empfängnisverhütende Methode	contraceptive method
Empfängnisverhütung	contraception
endgültige Nachkommenschaft	completed fertility

German	English
endogen	endogenous (of a death)
Enthaltsamkeit, periodische	rhythm method
Enthaltung, moralische	moral restraint
Entvölkerung	depopulation
Entwicklungsland	less developed country
Epidemie	epidemic, n.
epidemische Krankheit	epidemic, n.
Erblichkeit	heredity
erfasste Person	(census) respondent
Ergänzung	follow-up, n.
Ergänzung, fortlaufende	follow-up, n.
Ergebniss, bearbeitetes	refined figure
Erhebung	enumeration
Erkrankungshäufigkeit	incidence rate; morbidity
Erkrankungsziffer	incidence rate
Erwachsener	adult, n., m.
erwerbslos	unemployed, adj.
Erwerbsloser	unemployed, n., m.
Erwerbspersonen	economically active population
erwerbstätig	employed
Erzeugung	reproduction
ethnische Gruppe	ethnic group
Eugenik	eugenics
Existenzminimum (physiologisches)	subsistence level
exogen	exogenous (of a death)
Extrapolation	extrapolation
Familie	family
Familienbeihilfe	family allowance
Familiengrösse	family size
Familienkern	nuclear family
Familienplanung	family planning
Familienstand	marital status
Fehlgeburt	abortion
Flächenstichprobe	area sampling

German	English
Flecken	hamlet
Flüchtling	refugee
Fluktuation	fluctuation
Formblatt	form, n.
fortlaufende Ergänzung	follow-up, n.
Fortzug	departure (of emigrants)
Fötalsterblichkeit	fetal mortality
Fötus	fetus
Fragebogen	questionnaire
Frau	woman
Fruchtabgang	miscarriage
Fruchtbarkeit	fertility
Fruchtbarkeit einer Kohorte	cohort fertility
Fruchtbarkeit eines Jahrgangs	cohort fertility
Fruchtbarkeit (physiologische)	fecundity
Fruchtbarkeitsrate	fertility rate
Fruchtbarkeitsziffer	fertility rate
Frühgeburt	premature birth; prematurity of births
Frühsterblichkeit der Säuglinge	neonatal mortality
Gebärmutter	uterus
Gebiet	area; territory
geboren, im Ausland	foreign-born, adj.
geboren, im Inland	native-born, adj.
Geborenenhäufigkeit	fertility
Geborenenüberschuss	natural increase
Geborenenziffer	birth rate
Geburt	birth
Geburt, Lebenserwartung bei der	life expectancy at birth; mean length of life
Geburt, Ordnungszahl der	birth order
Geburt, Staatsangehörigkeit bei der	national origin
Geburt, verfrühte	premature birth
Geburtenabstand	birth interval; spacing (of births), n.
Geburtenbeschränkung	birth control
Geburtenfolge	birth order; parity

German	English
Geburtenkontrolle	birth control
Geburtenrate	birth rate
Geburtenregelung	family planning
Geburtenüberschuss	natural increase
Geburtenziffer	birth rate
Geburtlichkeit	fertility
geburtsnahe Sterblichkeit	perinatal mortality
Genauigkeit	accuracy
Genetik	genetics
Generation	generation
Generation, fiktive	synthetic cohort
Generationsdauer (durchschnittliche)	length of a generation
geographische Mobilität	geographical mobility
geographische Verteilung	geographical distribution
geometrisches Mittel	geometric mean
Geriatrie	geriatrics
Gerontologie	gerontology
Gesamtfruchtbarkeit, Index der	total fertility rate
Gesamtfruchtbarkeitsrate	total fertility rate
Gesamtzahl der durchlebten Jahre	total years lived
geschichtete Stichprobe	stratified sampling
Geschlecht	sex
Geschlecht und nach Altersgruppen, Ziffer nach dem	sex-age-specific rate
geschlechts- und altersspezifische Rate	sex-age-specific rate
Geschlechtsproportion	sex ratio
Geschlechtsverhältnis	sex ratio
Geschlechtsverkehr	coitus; sexual intercourse
Geschwister	siblings
Gesellschaftsschicht	social class
Gesundheitswesen, öffentliches	public health
Gesundheitswesen, staatliches	public health
Gewicht	(statistical) weight
gewogener Durchschnitt	weighted average; weighted mean

German	English
gewogenes arithmetisches Mittel	weighted mean
gezählte Person	(census) respondent
glätten (einer Kurve)	smoothing (of a curve)
Glaubensbekenntnis	religion
Glaubensgemeinschaft	(religious) denomination
Gliederungszahl	proportion
Grossrechenanlage (elektronische)	(electronic) computer
Grossstadt	city
Grundrichtung	trend
Grundschulausbildung	primary education
Grundzahl	number, n.; figure, n.
Gruppe	group(ing)
Gruppe, ethnische	ethnic group
Gruppe, sozio-ökonomische	socio-economic group
Gruppe, sozio-professionelle	socio-economic group
gruppieren	classify
Gymnasial- und Realschulausbildung	secondary education
Häufigkeitskoeffizient	rate
Häufigkeitsverteilung	(frequency) distribution
Häufigkeitsziffer	rate
häufigster Wert	mode
Häufung runder Zahlen	heaping; bunching
Hauptrichtung	trend
Hauptstadt	capital (city)
Haushalt	household
Haushaltsmitglied	member of a household
Haushaltsvorstand	head of a household
Häuserblock	block, n.
Hauswirt	landlord, m.
Hautfarbe	(skin) color
Heimatvertriebener	refugee, m.
Heiratshäufigkeit	nuptiality
Heiratsrate	marriage rate
Heiratsziffer	marriage rate

178

German	English
Hemmung, präventive	preventive check
Hemmung, repressive	positive check
Herkunft, nationale	national origin
Hervorbringung	reproduction
Hochschulausbildung	higher education
Index	index
Indikator	indicator
Individuum	individual
im Inland geboren	native-born, adj.
Inländer	native-born, n., m.
Interpolation	interpolation
Interviewer	interviewer, m.
intra-uterin Pessar	intra-uterine device; IUD
intrauterine Sterblichkeit	fetal mortality
Jahre, Gesamtzahl der durchlebten	total years lived
Jahrgang	cohort
Jahrgangs, Fruchtbarkeit eines	cohort fertility
Jugendalter	adolescence
Jugendlicher	adolescent, n., m.
jugendliches Alter	adolescence
junges Mädchen	adolescent, n., f.
Junggeselle	bachelor
Junggesellin	spinster
Jüngling	adolescent, n., m.
Kappe, Cervix	cervical cap; pessary; diaphragm
Kartogram	graph
Kennzeichen	characteristic; attribute
Kernfamilie	nuclear family
Kinder	offspring; progeny
Kinder, abhängige	dependent children
Kinder-Frauenziffer	child-woman ratio
Kinder, unversorgte	dependent children
Kinderbeihilfe	family allowance; family subsidy
Kindergeld	family allowance; family subsidy

179

German	English
Kinderzulage	family allowance; family subsidy
Klasse	group
klassifizieren	classify
Kleinkind	infant
Klimakterium	climacteric; menopause
Klumpenauswahl	cluster sampling
Kohabitation	cohabitation
Kohorte	cohort
Kohorte, Fruchtbarkeit einer	cohort fertility
Koitus	coitus
Kombinationstabelle	cross-tabulation
Konfession	(religious) denomination
Konkubinat	consensual union; concubinage
Kontrazeption	contraception
kontrazeptive Methode	contraceptive method
kontrazeptive Pille	contraceptive pill
kontrazeptives Mittel	contraceptive, n.
Kontrazeptivum, orales	oral contraceptive
Konurbation	standard metropolitan area; agglomeration; conurbation
Konzeption	conception
Krankenbestandsziffer	prevalence rate
Krankheit	disease
Krankheit, epidemische	epidemic, n.
kulturelle Anpassung	acculturation
Land	country
Land, unterentwickeltes	underdeveloped country; less developed country
ländlich	rural
Landwirtschaft, Berufszugehörige der	farm population; agricultural population
landwirtschaftliche Bevölkerung	agricultural population; farm population
Lebendgeburt	live birth
Lebensdauer, durchschnittliche	mean length of life
Lebensdauer, mittlere	median length of life

German	English
Lebensdauer, normale	longevity; length of life
Lebensdauer, wahrscheinliche	probable length of life
Lebenserwartung	life expectancy; expectation of life
Lebenserwartung bei der Geburt	life expectancy at birth; mean length of life
Lebenserwartung der Neugeborenen	life expectancy at birth; mean length of life
lebensfähig	viable (of a fetus)
Lebenshaltung, Höhe der	level of living; standard of living
Lebenshaltungsniveau	level of living; standard of living
Lebensspanne	life span
Lebensstandard	standard of living; level of living
ledig	single
ledig, nicht	ever married, adj.
des Lesens und Schreibens kundige Person	literate person
Locher	punch, n.
Lochkarte	punch card
Lochmaschine	punch, n.
lückenhafte Registrierung	underregistration
Mädchen, junges	adolescent, n., f.
Mann	man
männlichen Geschlechts, Person	male, n.; man
Median	median, n.
Mehrlingsgeburt	multiple birth
Menarche	menarche
Menopause	menopause; climacteric
Menstruation	menstruation
Merkmal (artmässiges)	characteristic; attribute
Merkmal (qualitatives)	characteristic; attribute
Methode nach Ogino-Knaus	rhythm method; periodic abstinence
Mieter	tenant, m.
Minderheit	minority
Mittel, gewogenes arithmetisches	weighted mean; weighted average
Mittelwert	mean, n.
mittlere Abweichung	standard error
mittlere Abweichung (einfache)	mean deviation

German	English
mittlere Abweichung (quadratische)	standard deviation
mittlere Bevölkerung	mean population
mittlere Lebensdauer	median length of life; probable length of life
Mobilität	geographical mobility; spatial mobility
Mobilität, geographische	geographical mobility; spatial mobility
Mobilität, räumliche	spatial mobility; geographical mobility
Mobilität, soziale	social mobility
Modell	model, n.
Modus	mode
Monatsregel, erste	menarche
Monatszyklus	menstrual cycle
moralische Enthaltung	moral restraint
Morbidität	morbidity
Morbiditätsziffer	incidence rate
Mortalität	mortality
Mutterschaft	parenthood (of mother)
Muttersprache	mother tongue; native language
Müttersterblichkeit	maternal mortality
Nachkommen	offspring; progeny
Nachkommenschaft, endgültige	completed fertility
Nachwuchs	offspring; progeny
Natalität	natality
Nation	nation
nationale Herkunft	national origin
Nationalität	nationality
Naturalisation	naturalization
Naturalisierung	naturalization
natürlicher Bevölkerungsbewegung, Statistik der	vital statistics
Naturraum	natural area
negatives Wachstum	negative growth
Neonatalsterblichkeit	neonatal mortality
Netto-	net
Nettoreproduktionsrate	net reproduction rate

German	English
Nettowanderung	net migration
Neugeborenen, Lebenserwartung der	life expectancy at birth; mean length of life
nicht angegeben	not stated
nicht bezeichnet	not stated
nicht ledig	ever married, adj.
Nichtbeantwortung	nonresponse
Nichtsesshafter	vagrant, m.
Niederkunft, Ordnungszahl der	parity; birth order
Nomade	nomad, n.
Obdachloser	vagrant, m.
offene Bevölkerung	open population
Ogino-Knaus, Methode nach	rhythm method; periodic abstinence
ohne Angabe	unknown; not stated
Okklusivpessar	diaphragm; pessary
Okkupant	squatter, m.
Ökologie, soziale	human ecology
optimale Bevölkerung	optimum population; population optimum
orales Kontrazeptivum	oral contraceptive
Ordnungszahl der Geburt	birth order; parity
ortsanwesende Bevölkerung	de facto population; enumerated population
Ovulation	ovulation
Paar	(married) couple
Pendelwanderung	commuting, n.
Pendler	commuter, m.
Pensionsgast	boarder
perinatale Sterblichkeit	perinatal mortality
periodische Enthaltsamkeit	periodic abstinence; rhythm method
Person	person
Pessar	pessary; diaphragm
Pessar, intra-uterin	intra-uterine device; IUD
"Pille danach"	morning-after pill
Pille, kontrazeptive	contraceptive pill
Population (statistische)	population (statistical)
Post-Natalsterblichkeit	post-neonatal mortality

German	English
Post-Neonatalsterblichkeit	post-neonatal mortality
Präservativ	condom; sheath
präventive Hemmung	preventive check
Produktivität	productivity
provisorisch	provisional
Prozentsatz	percentage; percent
Prozentzahl	percentage; percent
Pubertät	puberty
quasi-stabile Bevölkerung	quasi-stable population
Quote	proportion
Radixbestand	radix (of a life table)
Rangfolge	birth order; parity
Rasse	race, n.
Rate	rate
Rate, reine	intrinsic rate; true rate
Rate, stabile	intrinsic rate; true rate
Rate, wahre	intrinsic rate; true rate
Raum	area; territory; region
räumliche Mobilität	geographical mobility; spatial mobility
räumliche Verteilung	geographical distribution; spatial distribution
Realschul- und Gymnasialausbildung	secondary education
Region	region
Registrierung	registration
Registrierung, lückenhafte	underregistration
reine Rate	intrinsic rate; true rate
reine Reproduktionsziffer	net reproduction rate
Religionsbekenntnis	religion
repressive Hemmung	positive check
Reproduktionsziffer, reine	net reproduction rate
Reproduktionsziffer, rohe	gross reproduction rate
Revolution, demographische	demographic revolution; demographic transition
Risiko	risk
roh	crude (of a rate); gross

German	English
rohe Daten	basic, crude, primary, raw data
rohe Reproduktionsziffer	gross reproduction rate
Rohergebnisse	basic, crude, primary, raw data
Rückwanderung	return migration; remigration
runde Zahl	round number
Rundfrage	survey, n.
Salpingektomie	salpingectomy
Säugen (anhaltendes)	lactation (prolonged)
Säugling	infant
Säuglinge, Frühsterblichkeit der	neonatal mortality
Säuglingssterblichkeit	infant mortality
schätzen	estimate, v.
Schätzung	estimate, n.
Schaubild	diagram
Scheidenschwämmchen	(contraceptive) sponge
Scheidung	divorce
Schicht, soziale	social class
Schichtung, soziale	social stratification
Schwangerschaft	pregnancy
Schwangerschaftsabbruch	induced abortion
Schwangerschaftsunterbrechung, künstliche	induced abortion
Schwankung	fluctuation
Seele	soul; individual
Segregation	segregation
Selbstausfüllung (eines Fragebogens)	self-enumeration
Selbstzählung	self-enumeration
Senilität	senility
Serie	series
Seuche	epidemic, n.
Sexualproportion	sex ratio
Sicherheitsgrenze	level of significance
signieren	code, v.
Signifikanzgrenze	level of significance
Signifikanzniveau	level of significance

German	English
Simulation	simulation
Sortiermaschine	sorter
soziale Ökologie	human ecology
soziale Schicht	social class
soziale Schichtung	social stratification
sozio-ökonomische Gruppe	socio-economic group
sozio-professionelle Gruppe	socio-economic group
Spät-Säuglingssterblichkeit	post-neonatal mortality
Spermatozoon	sperm
Spontanabortus	spontaneous abortion
Staat	state; nation
Staatsangehöriger	citizen, m.
Staatsangehörigkeit	nationality
Staatsangehörigkeit bei der Geburt	national origin
Staatsbürger	citizen, m.; subject, n., m.
Staatsbürgerschaft	nationality
stabile Rate	intrinsic rate; true rate
stabile Bevölkerung	stable population
Stadt	town
städtisch	urban
städtische Agglomeration	agglomeration; conurbation; standard metropolitan area
Stadtkern	central city
Standardabweichung	standard deviation
Standardbevölkerung	standard population
Standardfehler	standard error
standardisiert	standardized (of a rate)
Standardisierungsmethode, direkte	direct method of standardization
Standardisierungsmethode, indirekte	indirect method of standardization
stationäre Bevölkerung	stationary population
Statistik der natürlichen Bevölkerungsbewegung	vital statistics
Stellung	relationship (to head of a household)
Sterbefall	death

German	English
Sterberate	death rate
Sterbetafel	life table
Sterbetafel, abgekürzte	abridged life table
Sterbetafel, vollständige	complete life table
Sterbeurkunde	death certificate
Sterbewahrscheinlichkeit	probability of death
Sterbeziffer	death rate
Sterbeziffer nach Todesursache(n)	cause-specific mortality rate
Sterblichkeit	mortality
Sterblichkeit, differenzielle	differential mortality
Sterblichkeit, geburtsnahe	perinatal mortality
Sterblichkeit, intrauterine	fetal mortality
Sterblichkeit, perinatale	perinatal mortality
Sterilisation	sterilization
Sterilisation (des Mannes)	vasectomy
Sterilisierung	sterilization
Sterilität	sterility
Stichprobe	sample, n.
Stichprobe, geschichtete	stratified sample
Stichprobe, repräsentative	representative sample
Stichprobenerhebung	sample survey
Stichprobenfehler	sampling error
Stichprobenverfahren	sampling, n.
Streuung	scatter; dispersion; variation
Tabelle	table, n.
tabellieren	tabulate
Tafel	table, n.
Teilbevölkerung	subpopulation
Tod	death
Todesursache	cause of death
Todesursache(n), Sterbeziffer nach	cause-specific mortality rate
Totgeburt	stillbirth
Transformation, demographische	demographic transition

German	English
Trend	trend
Tubenligatur	tubal ligation
Überalterung	aging
Überbevölkerung	overpopulation
Übergang, demographischer	demographic transition
Überlebender	survivor, m.
Überlebenswahrscheinlichkeit	probability of survival
Übervölkerung	overpopulation
unbekannt	unknown
unehelich	illegitimate
Unehelichkeit	illegitimacy
Unfruchtbarkeit	sterility
Unfruchtbarmachung	sterilization
Unterbevölkerung	underpopulation
unterentwickeltes Land	underdeveloped country
Untererfassung	underenumeration
Untermieter	lodger, m.
Unterschied	difference
Unterstichprobe	subsample
Untervölkerung	underpopulation
unversorgte Kinder	dependent children
Uterus	uterus
Vagabund	vagrant, m.
Variable	variable, n.
Variationsbreite	range
Vaterschaft	parenthood (of father)
Veränderliche	variable, n.
verbessert	revised
Verbindung	union
Vererbung	heredity
Verhältniszahl	ratio
verheiratete Frau	married woman
verheirateter Mann	married man
Verjüngen	younging (of a population)

German	English
Verstädterung	urbanization
Verteilung	(frequency) distribution
Verteilung, geographische	geographical distribution; spatial distribution
Verteilung, räumliche	spatial distribution; geographical distribution
Vertreibung	forced migration
Vertriebener	displaced person, m.; refugee, m.
Vervollständigung	follow-up, n.
Verwandte	relatives; kin
Volk	nation; people
Volksgruppe	ethnic group
Volkszählung	census
Vordruck	form, n.
vorläufig	provisional
Vorort	suburb
Wachstum der Bevölkerung	population growth
Wachstum, negatives	negative growth; population decline
Wägungsfaktor	(statistical) weight
wahre Rate	true rate; intrinsic rate
wahrscheinliche Lebensdauer	probable length of life; median length of life
Wahrscheinlichkeit	probability
Wanderer	migrant, m.
Wanderung	migration; geographical mobility
Wanderung, internationale	international migration
Wanderungsbilanz	net migration
Wanderungssaldo	net migration
weiblichen Geschlechts, Person	female, n.; woman
Wert, dichtester	mode
Wert, häufigster	mode
Wiederaufnehmung	follow-up, n.
Wiederverheiratung	remarriage
Wirtschaftsabteilung	sector of the economy
Wirtschaftsentwicklung	economic development
Wirtschaftssektor	sector of the economy
Wirtschaftswachstum	economic growth

German	English
Wirtschaftszweig	sector of the economy
Wohnbevölkerung	de jure population; resident population
Wohnort, Person ohne festen	vagrant; person of no fixed abode
Wohnsitz	residence
Wohnung	dwelling unit
Zahl	number, n.; figure, n.
Zahl, abgeleitete	refined figure
Zahl, runde	round figure
Zahlen, Häufung runder	heaping; bunching
Zählbezirk	census tract
Zählblatt	schedule, n.
Zähler	enumerator, m.
Zählung	enumeration
Zeit, durchlebte	total years lived
Zeitreihe	time series
zentral	median, adj.
Zentralwert	median, n.
Zeugung	reproduction
Zufallsstichprobe	probability sample
Zuwanderung	arrival (of immigrants)
Zuzug	arrival (of immigrants)
Zwangsumsiedler	displaced person, m.
Zwangswanderung	forced migration

Japanese to English

Japanese	English
akanbō	baby; infant
antei jinkō	stable population
atsuryoku, jinkō	population pressure
bakkyohō	withdrawal; coitus interruptus
bokokugo	native language; mother tongue
boshūdan, fukuji	subpopulation
bunka henyō	acculturation
bunpu, chiriteki	geographical distribution
bunpu (dosū)	(frequency) distribution
bunpu han'i	range
bunpu, kūkanteki	spatial distribution
bunpu, nenrei	age distribution
bunri (kyojūchi no)	segregation
bunruiki	sorter (machine)
bunruisuru	classify
bunsan (do)	dispersion; scatter
bunseki	analysis
burroku	block, n.
byōki	disease
chakushō	conception
chakushutsu	legitimacy
chakushutsu no	legitimate
chiiki	area; region
chiiki chūshutsuhō	area sampling
chirabari	dispersion; scatter
chiriteki bunpu	geographical distribution
chiriteki idō	geographical mobility
chōju	length of life; longevity
chokusetsu hyōjunkahō	direct method of standardization
chōsa	survey, n.
chōsa, hyōhon	sample survey
chōsa, jikeishiki	self-enumeration
chōsa, jikishiki	self-enumeration
chōsa, kokusei	census

Japanese	English
chōsa ku, kokusei	census tract
chōsa kyakutai	subject, n.
chōsa more, tōroku jinkō no	underregistration
chōsa, tsuiseki	follow-up, n.
chōsahyō	form, n.; schedule, n.
chōsain	enumerator
chōsasha	enumerator
chūō seizon-ritsu	median length of life; probable length of life
chūōchi	median, n.
chūōno	median, adj.
chūshin toshi	central city
chūshutsu, hyōhon	sampling, n.
chūshutsuhō, chiiki	area sampling
chūshutsuhō, shūraku	cluster sampling
chūshutsuhō, sōka	stratified sampling
chūtō kyōiku	secondary education
chūzetsu	abortion
chūzetsu, jinkō ninshin	induced abortion
chūzetsuhō, seikō	coitus interruptus; withdrawal
daihyō hyōhon	representative sample
daitoshiken, hyōjun	standard metropolitan area
datai	abortion
denominēshon	denomination
densenbyō	epidemic, n.
denshi keisanki	computer (electronic)
dēta	data
dōikon	consensual union
dōji shusshō shūdan	cohort
dōka	assimilation
dōkō	trend
dokushin	single; never married
dokushin seikatsu	celibacy
dokushin (sha)	bachelor
dōsei	union

Japanese	English
dosū bunpu	frequency distribution
dōtokuteki yokusei	moral restraint
forō appu	follow-up, n.
fūfu	married couple
fugōkasura	code, v.
fuhō kyojūsha	squatter
fujin	woman
fujin kodomo hiritsu	child-woman ratio
fuku hyōhon	subsample
fukuji boshūdan	subpopulation
fukusan	multiple birth
fumei	unknown; not stated
funin shujutsu	sterilization
funinshō	sterility
fūsa jinkō	closed population
futsu (ritsu)	crude (of a rate)
fuyō jidō	dependent children
fuyōsha	dependent, n.
gaiinsei no (shiin)	exogenous (of a death)
gaikoku umare	foreign-born
gaisū	round number
gekkei	menstruation
gekkei heishi kikan	menopause; climacteric
gekkei shūki	menstrual cycle
gen-shiryō	primary data
genshō, jinkō	population decline; depopulation
genzai jinkō	de facto population
geshukunin	boarder
gōkei tokushu shusshō-ritsu	total fertility rate
gosa, hyōjun	standard error
gōsei kōhōto	synthetic cohort
gun	group
gurafu	graph
gurūpu	group

Japanese	English
haigū kankei	marital status; civil status
haigūsha	spouse
hairan	ovulation
han'i	range
heijunka	smoothing (of a curve)
heikatsuka	smoothing (of a curve)
heikin hensa	mean deviation
heikin jinkō	mean population
heikin jumyō	life expectancy at birth; mean length of life
heikin, kajū	weighted mean
heikin, kika	geometric mean
heikin no	mean, adj.; average, adj.
heikin yomei	life expectancy; expectation of life
heikinchi	mean, n.; average, n.
hendō	fluctuation; variation
hendō, keikō	trend
hen'i	variation
hen'isei	variability
hensa, heikin	mean deviation
hensa, hyōjun	standard deviation
hensū	variable, n.
hi	ratio
hichakushutsu	illegitimacy
hichakushutsu no	illegitimate
hichōsasha	subject, n.
hinin	contraception
hinin kigu	contraceptive, n.
hinin yaku, keikō	oral contraceptive
hininhō	contraceptive method
hininyō piru	contraceptive pill
hito	person; individual
hogaihō	extrapolation
hokanhō	interpolation
hongoku umare	native-born

195

Japanese	English
hōrōsha	vagrant, n.; person of no fixed abode
hosei sūji	refined figure
hoseisareta	corrected
hyakubun-ritsu	percentage
hyō	table, n.
hyōhon	sample, n.
hyōhon chōsa	sample survey
hyōhon chūshutsu	sampling, n.
hyōhon, daihyō	representative sample
hyōhon, fuku	subsample
hyōhon gosa	sampling error
hyōhon, kakuritsu	probability sample
hyōjun daitoshiken	standard metropolitan area
hyōjun gosa	standard error
hyōjun hensa	standard deviation
hyōjun jinkō	standard population
hyōjunka (ritsu)	standardized (of a rate)
hyōjunkahō, chokusetsu	direct method of standardization
hyōjunkahō, kansetsu	indirect method of standardization
hyōka, kashō (chōsa kekka no)	underenumeration
hyōshiki	characteristic; attribute
ichiji genjūsha	transient, n.
iden	heredity
idengaku	genetics
idō, chiriteki	geographical mobility
idō, jinkō	migration
idō, jun-jinkō	net migration
idō, kikan	return migration; remigration
idō, kokunai jinkō	internal migration
idō, kokusai	international migration
idō, kūkanteki	spatial mobility
idō, shakai	social mobility
idō, tsūkin	commuting, n.

Japanese	English
ijū	migration
ijū, kokusai	international migration
ijū, kyōsei	forced migration
ijūsha	migrant
imin	migration
imin, shukkoku	emigration
inseki	kin; relatives
inyūmin	immigration
iro (hifu no)	color (of skin)
jakunenka (jinkō no)	younging (of a population)
jido, fuyō	dependent children
jikeiretsu	time series
jikeishiki chōsa	self-enumeration
jikishiki chōsa	self-enumeration
jinbutsu	soul; individual
jinkō	population
jinkō, antei	stable population
jinkō atsuryoku	population pressure
jinkō dōtai tōkei	vital statistics
jinkō, fūsa	closed population
jinkō gakusha	demographer
jinkō genshō	population decline; depopulation
jinkō, genzai	de facto population
jinkō, heikin	mean population
jinkō, hyōjun	standard population
jinkō idō	migration
jinkō idō, kokunai	internal migration
jinkō, jōjū	de jure population
jinkō, jun-antei	quasi-stable population
jinkō, kaihō	open population
jinkō, kajō	overpopulation
jinkō kakumei	demographic transition
jinkō, kashō	underpopulation

Japanese	English
jinkō, katsudō	economically active population
jinkō mitsudo	population density
jinkō ninshin chūzetsu	induced abortion
jinkō, nōgyō	agricultural population
jinkō, nōka	farm population
jinkō piramiddo	population pyramid
jinkō seisaku	population policy
jinkō, seishi	stationary population
jinkō suikei	population projection
jinkō tekido	population optimum
jinkō, tekido	optimum population
jinkō tenkan	demographic transition
jinkō tōkei	population statistics
jinkō tōroku	population register
jinkō, tsūkin	commuter
jinkō yosoku	population forecast
jinkō zōka	population growth
jinkō zōka, mainasu	negative growth; population decline
jinkōgaku	demography
jinshu	race, n.
jissa	enumeration
jiyūkon	free union
jōjū jinkō	de jure population
jūkyo	dwelling unit; residence
jūmin tōroku	registration
jumyō	longevity; length of life; life span
jumyō, heikin	life expectancy at birth; mean length of life
jun	net, adj.
jun-antei jinkō	quasi-stable population
jun-jinkō idō	net migration
jun-saiseisan ritsu	net reproduction rate
junyū kikan (enchō-shita)	lactation (prolonged)
jusei	fertilization
jūsho futeishā	vagrant; person of no fixed abode

Japanese	English
jutai	conception
jūzoku shisū	dependency ratio
kādo, panchi	punch card
kādo, senkō	punch card
kahensei	variability
kaihō jinkō	open population
kaikyū, shakai	social class
kaisō, shakai	social class
kaitōsha (kokusei chōsa)	respondent (census)
kajō jinkō	overpopulation
kajū heikin	weighted mean
kajūchi	weight (statistical)
kaku kazoku	nuclear family
kakumaku (pessarī)	diaphragm; pessary
kakumei, jinkō	demographic transition
kakuri	segregation
kakuritsu	probability
kakuritsu hyōhon	probability sample
kakuritsu, shibō	probability of death
kankaku (shusshō no)	spacing (of births), n.
kanketsu shusshō-ryoku	completed fertility
kansetsu hyōjunkahō	indirect method of standardization
kansoku seimeihyō	abridged life table
kansoku seishi jinkōhyō	abridged life table
kanzen seimeihyō	complete life table
karino	provisional
kashō hyōka (chōsa kekka no)	underenumeration
kashō jinkō	underpopulation
kashō tōroku	underregistration
katei no	provisional
katsudō jinkō	active population
kazoku	family
kazoku, kaku	nuclear family
kazoku keikaku	family planning

Japanese	English
kazoku kibo	family size
kazoku teate	family allowance; family subsidy
kazu	number, n.; figure, n.
keikō hendō	trend
keikō hinin yaku	oral contraceptive
keiretsu	series
keizai hatten	economic development
keizai seichō	economic growth
kekkon	marriage; nuptiality; union
kekkon jizoku kikan	duration of marriage
kijun	base, n.
kika	naturalization
kika heikin	geometric mean
kikan idō	return migration; remigration
kiken-ritsu	risk; chance
kikon danshi	married man
kikon joshi	married woman
kikon no	ever married, adj.
kinyoku seikatsu	celibacy
kiso shiryō	basic data
kodomo	child; offspring
kōgai	suburb
kōhōto	cohort
kōhōto, gōsei	synthetic cohort
kōhōto shussan-ryoku	cohort fertility
kōhōto shusshō-ryoku	cohort fertility
kojin	individual; person
kōki shinseiji shibō-ritsu	post-neonatal mortality
kokka	state, n.; nation
kokumin	people
kokunai jinkō idō	internal migration
kokusai idō	international migration
kokusai ijū	international migration

Japanese	English
kokusei chōsa	census
kokusei chōsa ku	census tract
kokuseki	nationality
kondōmu	condom
kon'in	marriage; nuptiality
kon'in kikan	duration of marriage
kon'in-ritsu	marriage rate
konpyūtā	computer (electronic)
kōreika	aging, n.
koshū eisei	public health
kōtō kyōiku	higher education
koyōsha	employed
kūkanteki bunpu	spatial distribution; geographical distribution
kūkanteki idō	spatial mobility; geographical mobility
kumi	set, n.
kuni	country
kurasutā sanpuringu	cluster sampling
kurosu shūkei	cross-tabulation
kyōdai	siblings
kyōiku, chūtō	secondary education
kyōiku, kōtō	higher education
kyōiku, shotō	primary education
kyojūsha	inhabitant
kyojūsha, fuhō	squatter
kyōsei ijū	forced migration
machi	town
magarinin	lodger
mainasu jinkō zōka	negative growth; population decline
mainoritii	minority
median	median, n.
mekake kankei	concubinage
mensetsusha	interviewer
mikon	single; never married
mikon joshi	spinster

Japanese	English
minzoku	nation
minzoku, shosū	minority
minzoku shūdan	ethnic group
mitsudo, jinkō	population density
moderu	model, n.
mōdo	mode
mōdo no	modal
mokei	model, n.
mōningu āfutā piru	morning-after pill
mukaitō	nonresponse
munōryoku	disability
mura	village
naiinsei no (shiin)	endogenous (of a death)
nama no shiryō	raw data
nanmin	displaced person; refugee
nenrei	age
nenrei-betsu tokushu-ritsu	age-specific rate
nenrei bunpu	age distribution
nenrei-gun	age group(ing)
nenrei kaikyū (seimeihyō no)	radix (of a life table)
nenrei kōzō	age structure
nenreisō	age bracket
ningen seitaigaku	human ecology
ninsanpu shibō-ritsu	maternal mortality; puerperal mortality
ninshin	conception; pregnancy; gestation
ninshin chūzetsu, jinkō	induced abortion
ninshin kanōsei	fecundability
ninshin nōryoku	fecundability
ninshin ryoku	fecundity
nōgyō jinkō	agricultural population
nōka jinkō	farm population
nōson no	rural
nyūji	infant; baby
nyūji shibō-ritsu	infant mortality

Japanese	English
nyūkoku (imin no)	arrival (of immigrants)
on'na	female, n.
otoko	male, n.; man
otona	adult, n.
ōya	landlord
oyadearu koto	parenthood
panchi kādo	punch card
pāsento	percent
pessarī	diaphragm; pessary
piramiddo, jinkō	population pyramid
piru	contraceptive pill; oral contraceptive
piru, hininyō	contraceptive pill; oral contraceptive
piru, mōningu āfutā	morning-after pill
piru, seikōgo fukuyō	post-coital contraceptive
radikkusu	radix (of a life table)
rankan kessatsu	tubal ligation
rankan setsudan	salpingectomy
ranshi	ovum
ribyō-ritsu	morbidity
rikan-ritsu	incidence rate
rikon	divorce
ritsu	rate
rizumuhō	rhythm method
rōjinbyōgaku	geriatrics
rōka	aging, n.
rōnen	old age
rōnengaku	gerontology
rōnenka	aging, n.
rōrei	old age; senility
rōreika	aging, n.
ryōdo	territory
ryōiki	region
ryōshin	parents
ryūzan	abortion; miscarriage

Japanese	English
ryūzan, shizen	spontaneous abortion
sābei	survey, n.
sabetsu shibō-ritsu	differential mortality
sai	difference
saihinchi	mode
saihinchi no	modal
saikon	remarriage
saiseisan	reproduction
saiseisan-ritsu, jun-	net reproduction rate
saiseisan-ritsu, so-	total fertility rate
saiseisan-ritsu, sō-	gross reproduction rate
sangyō	industry; sector of the economy
sanji seigen	birth control
sanpudo	dispersion; scatter, n.
sanpuringu	sampling, n.
sanpuringu, kurasutā	cluster sampling
sedai	generation
sedai kankaku	length of a generation
sei	sex
sei-nenrei-betsu-tokushu-ritsu	sex-age-specific rate
seieki	sperm
seihi	sex ratio
seihyō suru	tabulate
seijin	adult, n.
seikakusa	accuracy
seikan setsujo shujutsu	vasectomy
seikatsu, dokushin	celibacy
seikatsu iji suijun	subsistence level
seikatsu, kinyoku	celibacy
seikatsu suijun	level of living; standard of living
seikō	coitus; sexual intercourse
seikō chūzetsuhō	coitus interruptus; withdrawal
seikōgo fukuyō piru	postcoital contraceptive
seimeihyō	life table
seimeihyō, kansoku	abridged life table

Japanese	English
seimeihyō, kanzen	complete life table
seimeiryoku no aru (taiji ga)	viable (of a fetus)
seinen	adolescent, n.
seinenki	adolescence
seisaku, jinkō	population policy
seisanryoku	productivity
seisansei	productivity
seishi jinkō	stationary population
seishi jinkōhyō, kansoku	abridged life table
seisō, shakai	social stratification
seizan	live birth
seizan-ritsu	probability of survival
seizon kikan	length of life; longevity
seizon nensū	total years lived
seizon-ritsu	probability of survival
seizon-ritsu, chūō	median length of life; probable length of life
seizonsha	survivor
sekkyokuteki yokusei	positive check
senkō	punch, n.
senkō kādo	punch card
sensasu	census
sensasu torakuto	census tract
setai	household
setai-jin'in	member of a household
setai-nushi	head of a household
setaiin	member of a household
setto	set, n.
shakai idō	social mobility
shakai kaikyū	social class
shakai kaisō	social class
shakai-keizaiteki shūdan	socio-economic group
shakai seisō	social stratification
shakuchinin	tenant
shakuyanin	tenant
shi	city

205

Japanese	English
shibō	death
shibō kakuritsu	probability of death
shibō-ritsu	death rate; mortality
shibō-ritsu, kōki shinseiji	post-neonatal mortality
shibō-ritsu, ninsanpu	maternal mortality; puerperal mortality
shibō-ritsu, nyūji	infant mortality
shibō-ritsu, sabetsu	differential mortality
shibō-ritsu, shiinbetsu	cause-specific mortality rate
shibō-ritsu, shinseiji	neonatal mortality
shibō-ritsu, shūsanki	perinatal mortality
shibō-ritsu, taiji	fetal mortality
shibō-ryoku	mortality
shibō shōmeisho	death certificate
shihyō	indicator
shiin	cause of death
shiinbetsu shibō-ritsu	cause-specific mortality rate
shikyū	uterus; womb
shikyū keikanbō	cervical cap; diaphragm; pessary
shikyūnai hinin kigu (sōchi)	intra-uterine device; IUD
shikyūnai hinin sōchi	intra-uterine device; IUD
shimin	citizen
shinrui	relatives; kin
shinsei-ritsu	intrinsic rate; true rate
shinseiji shibō-ritsu	neonatal mortality
shinseiji shibō-ritsu, kōki	post-neonatal mortality
shippei	disease
shiryō	data
shiryō, kiso	basic data
shiryō, nama no	raw data
shiryō, so-	crude data
shishunki	puberty
shison	progeny; offspring
shisū	index
shitsugyō chū no	unemployed, adj.
shitsugyōsha	unemployed, n.

Japanese	English
shitsumonshi	questionnaire
shizan	stillbirth
shizen chiiki	natural area
shizen ryūzan	spontaneous abortion
shizen zōka	natural increase
shō-sonraku	hamlet
shochō	menarche
shokugyō	occupation
shōkyokuteki yokusei	preventive check
shoshutsu	illegitimacy
shoshutsu no	illegitimate
shosū minzoku	minority
shotō kyōiku	primary education
shūdan	group
shūdan, dōji shusshō	cohort
shūdan, minzoku	ethnic group
shūdan, shakai-keizaiteki	socio-economic group
shūha	denomination
shūkei	count, n.
shūkei, kurosu	cross-tabulation
shūkei suru	tabulate
shūkihō	periodic abstinence
shukkoku imin	emigration
shukkoku (imin no)	departure (of emigrants)
shūkyō	religion
shumirēshon	simulation
shūraku chūshutsuhō	cluster sampling
shūsanki shibō-ritsu	perinatal mortality
shūseki	heaping; bunching
shussan	birth
shussan nōryoku	fertility; natality
shussan-ryoku	fertility; natality
shussan-ryoku, kōhōto	cohort fertility
shussei	birth; live birth

Japanese	English
shusshin koku	national origin
shusshō	birth; live birth
shusshō chitsujo (jun'i)	birth order
shusshō chōsetsu	birth control
shusshō kankaku	birth interval
shusshō paritii	parity
shusshō-ritsu	birth rate
shusshō-ritsu, gōkei tokushu	total fertility rate
shusshō-ritsu, sō-	fertility rate
shusshō-ryoku	fertility; natality
shusshō-ryoku, kanketsu	completed fertility
shusshō-ryoku, kōhōto	cohort fertility
shusshō shūdan, dōji	cohort
shuto	capital (city)
sō	gross
so-saiseisan-ritsu	total fertility rate
sō-saiseisan-ritsu	gross reproduction rate
so-shiryō	crude data
sō-shusshō-ritsu	fertility rate
sōka chūshutsuhō	stratified sampling
sōzan	premature birth
suikei, jinkō	population projection
suitei	estimate, n.
suiteichi	estimate, n.
suiteisuru	estimate, v.
sūji	figure, n.; number, n.
sūji, hosei	refined figure
sukuwōtā	squatter
suponji (hinin yōgu)	sponge (contraceptive)
taiji	fetus
taiji shibō-ritsu	fetal mortality
tanki taizaisha	transient, n.
tanshin	single; never married
teikaihatsu koku	less developed country; underdeveloped country

Japanese	English
teiseisareta	revised
tekido jinkō	optimum population
tekido, jinkō	population optimum
tenkan, jinkō	demographic transition
tōkei, jinkō	population statistics
torendo	trend
tōroku, jinkō	population register
tōroku jinkō no chōsa more	underregistration
tōroku, jūmin	registration
tōroku, kashō	underregistration
tōsa	survey, n.
toshi	city
toshi, chūshin	central city
toshi no	urban
toshika	urbanization
tsuiseki chōsa	follow-up, n.
tsūkin idō	commuting, n.
tsūkin jinkō	commuter
tsuzuki-gara (setai-nushi ni taisuru)	relationship (to head of household)
wariai	proportion
yanushi	owner
yomei, heikin	life expectancy; expectation of life
yomikakidekiru hito	literate person
yosoku, jinkō	population forecast
yūbokumin	nomad
yubyō-ritsu	prevalence rate
yūi suijun	level of significance
yūseigaku	eugenics
zōka, jinkō	population growth
zōka, mainasu jinkō	negative growth; population decline
zōka, shizen	natural increase
zokusei	attribute; characteristic
zuhyō	diagram

Chinese (Pin-yin) to English

Chinese (Pin-yin)	English
bai fen bi	percentage
bai fen zhi . . .	. . . percent
bao xian tao	condom; sheath
bei diao cha de dui xiang	subject, n.
ben guo sheng	native-born
bi li	proportion; ratio
bi yun	contraception
bi yun fa	contraceptive method
bi yun gong ju	contraceptive, n. (barrier)
bi yun wan yao	contraceptive pill
bi yun yao wu	contraceptive, n. (pill)
bian shu	variable, n.
bian yi	variation; variability
biao	table, n.
biao shi	form, n.
biao zhun du hui qu	standard metropolitan area; agglomeration; conurbation
biao zhun hua	standardized (of a rate)
biao zhun pian cha	standard deviation
biao zhun ren kou	standard population
biao zhun wu cha	standard error
bo dong	fluctuation
bu ren	sterility
bu ru qi (yan chang)	lactation (prolonged)
can fei	disability
cha bie si wang	differential mortality
cha ji	enumeration
cha ji pian di	underenumeration
cha ji ren kou	de facto population; enumerated population
cha ji yuan	enumerator
cha yi	difference
chan fu si wang	maternal mortality; puerperal mortality
chang zhu ren kou	de jure population; resident population
chen hou wan	morning-after pill
cheng ren	adult, n.
cheng shi	city
cheng zhen	urban

Chinese (Pin-yin)	English
chu chao	menarche
chu sheng lü	birth rate
chu sheng sheng ming yu qi zhi	life expectancy at birth
chun	net
ci kai fa guo jia	less developed country; underdeveloped country
ci ren kou	subpopulation
ci yang ben	subsample
cu (lü)	crude (of a rate)
cu zai sheng chan zhi lü	gross reproduction rate
cu zi liao	crude data
cun huo gai lü	probability of survival
cun huo zhe	survivor
da ka	punch card
da kong	punch, n.
dai biao yang ben	representative sample
dan shen	single
dao da	arrival (of immigrants)
dao de jie zhi	moral restraint
deng ji	registration
deng ji guo di	underregistration
di duan	block, n.
di li fen bu	geographical distribution; spatial distribution
di li yi dong	geographical mobility; spatial mobility
di qu	area
di qu xuan yang	area sampling
di yu	territory
di zhu	landlord
dian nao	(electronic) computer
dian xing	model, n.
diao cha	survey
diao cha biao	questionnaire; schedule, n.
du shen	bachelor
du shen sheng huo	celibacy
du shi	city, municipality
du shi hua	urbanization
dui ji	heaping; bunching

Chinese (Pin-yin)	English
duo sheng yu	multiple birth
duo shu de	modal
duo tai	abortion
fa bing lü	incidence rate
fa ze	code, v.
fan zhi	reproduction
fang shi	mode
fang wen biao	schedule, n.
fang wen yuan	interviewer
fang zhi xing yi zhi	preventive check
fen ceng xuan yang	stratified sample
fen bu	(frequency) distribution
fen lei	classify
feng bi ren kou	closed population
feng xi	analysis
fu fu	(married) couple
fu mu	parents
fu mu shen fen	parenthood
fu nü	female, n.; woman
fu se	(skin) color
fu shu cheng zhang	negative growth
gao deng jiao yu	higher education
ge li	segregation
ge ren	individual
gong gong wei sheng	public health
gong min	citizen
gong ye	industry
gou wai sheng	foreign-born
gu ji	estimate, n. and v.; estimation
gu you lü	intrinsic rate; true rate
guan xi	relationship (to head of household)
gui hua	naturalization
gui lei ji	(machine) sorter
guo ji	nationality

Chinese (Pin-yin)	English
guo ji qian yi	international migration
guo jia	country; nation; state
guo ke	transient, n.
guo nei qian yi	internal migration
guo ren	people (nation)
guo sheng ren kou	overpopulation
hai fu bi	child-woman ratio
hai mian	(contraceptive) sponge
han hua	acculturation
he fa	legitimacy
he fa di	legitimate
he xin jia ting	nuclear family
hou dai	offspring; progeny
hu kou	household
hu yuan	member of a household
hu zhang	head of a household
hu zhu	head of a household
huai yun	conception; pregnancy; gestation
hui gui qian yi	return migration; remigration
hun yin	nuptiality
hun yin zhuang kuang	marital status; civil status; conjugal status
huo sheng yu	live birth
ji ben zi liao	basic data
ji bing	disease; morbidity
ji he ping jun shu	geometric mean
ji hui	chance
ji ji xing yi zhi	positive check
ji ju zhe	boarder; lodger
ji shu (sheng ming biao)	radix (of a life table)
ji ti xuan yang	cluster sampling
ji yu yang ben	probability sample
ji zhun	base, n.
jia quan ping jun shu	weighted mean; weighted average
jia ting	family

Chinese (Pin-yin)	English
jia ting bu zhu	family allowance
jia ting da xiao	family size
jia ting ji hua	family planning
jia ting jing tie	family allowance
jian ge	spacing (of births), n.
jian jie fa biao zhun hua	indirect method of standardization
jian yao sheng ming biao	abridged life table
jiao hu lie biao	cross-tabulation
jiao pai	(religious) denomination
jiao zheng di	revised; corrected
jie guo hun	ever married
jie he	union
jie hun	marriage
jie hun jiu du	duration of marriage
jie hun lü	marriage rate
jing ji bu men	sector of the economy
jing ji cheng zhang	economic growth
jing ji fa zhan	economic development
jing qi	menstrual cycle
jing qian yi	net migration
jing xi shu zi	refined figure
jing zhi ren kou	stationary population
jing zai sheng chan lü	net reproduction rate
jing zi	sperm
jiu ye	employed
ju min	inhabitant
ju zhu ren kou	de jure population; resident population
juan shu	depenent, n.
juan shu zi nü	dependent children
jue yu	sterilization
jun yun hua	smoothing (of a curve)
kai fang ren kou	open population
ke neng lü	probability
ke yu di (tai er)	viable (of a fetus)
kou fu bi yun yao	oral contraceptive

Chinese (Pin-yin)	English
lao chu nü	spinster
lao dong ren kou	economically active population
lao hua	aging
lao nian	old age
lao nian bing xue	geriatrics
lao nian xue	gerontology
li hun	divorce
lie biao	tabulate
liu lang zhe	vagrant; person of no fixed abode
liu xing bing	epidemic, n.
liu xing lü	prevalence rate
lü	rate
luan zi	ovum
min zu	ethnic group
mo ni	simulation
mo xing	model, n.
mu yu	mother tongue; native language
nan	male, n.; man
nan min	refugee
nei cha fa	interpolation
nei fa di	endogenous (of deaths)
nian bie lü	age-specific rate
nian ling	age
nian ling cong*	age group
nian ling fen bu	age distribution
nian ling jie gou	age structure
nian ling zu	age group
nian qing hua	younging (of a population)
nong cun	rural
nong ye ren kou	agricultural population
pai luan	ovulation
pei ou	spouse

*Translates the English but is not generally used.

Chinese (Pin-yin)	English
pei tai	fetus
pin ju	concubinage
ping jun di	mean, adj.; average, adj.
ping jun di cha shu	mean deviation
ping jun shu	mean, n.; average, n.
pu cha	census
pu cha qu	census tract
qian yi	migration
qiang po qian yi	forced migration
qin shu	relatives; kin
qing chun qi	puberty
qing kuang bu ming wu da	unknown; not stated
qing shao nian	adolescent
qing yuan jie he	consensual union
qu shi	trend
qu yu	region
quan ju	range
quan shu	(statistical) weight
qun ji	heaping; bunching
ren	person
ren gong duo tai	induced abortion
ren kou	population
ren kou bian geng	demographic transition
ren kou deng ji	population register
ren kou ge ming	demographic revolution; demographic transition
ren kou jian di	depopulation; population decline
ren kou jin zi ta	population pyramid
ren kou mi du	population density
ren kou pian di	underpopulation
ren kou tong ji	population statistics
ren kou tong ji xue	demography
ren kou tong ji xue zhe	demographer
ren kou ya li	population pressure

Chinese (Pin-yin)	English
ren kou yu ce	population forecast; population projection
ren kou zeng zhang	population growth
ren kou zheng ce	population policy
ren shen	gestation; pregnancy
ren wen sheng tai	human ecology
san bu	dispersion; scatter, n.
shao shu min zu	minority
she hui jie ceng	social stratification
she hui jie ji	social class
she hui jing ji tuan ti	socio-economic group
she hui liu dong	social mobility
sheng chan li	productive forces
sheng chan neng li sheng chan lü	productivity
sheng cun zhong nian shu	total years lived
sheng huo cheng du	standard of living
sheng huo shui ping	level of living
sheng ji du	subsistence level
sheng ming biao	life table; mortality table
sheng ming fu du	life span
sheng ming ke neng chang du	probable length of life
sheng ming ping jun du	mean length of life
sheng ming tong ji	vital statistics
sheng ming yu qi zhi	life expectancy; expectation of life
sheng ming zhong wei du	median length of life
sheng xu	parity
sheng yu	birth
sheng yu jian ge	birth interval
sheng yu jie zhi	birth control
sheng yu li	fertility; natality
sheng yu lü	fertility rate
sheng zhi li	fecundability; fecundity
sheng zi liao	raw data
shi dai	generation
shi dai chang du	length of a generation

Chinese (Pin-yin)	English
shi du ren kou	population optimum; optimum population
shi jian shu lie	time series
shi jiao	suburb
shi zi zhe	literate person
shou du	capital (city)
shou ming	longevity; length of life
shou tai	fertilization
shou zu	siblings
shu jing guan qie chu shu	vasectomy
shu lie	series
shu luan guan jie zha	tubal ligation
shu luan guan qie chu shu	salpingectomy
shu mu	count, n.; number, n.
shuzi, tu biao	figure, n.
shuai lao	senility
si chan	stillbirth
si sheng	illegitimacy
si sheng di	illegitimate
si sheng zi	illegitimate child
si wang	death; mortality
si wang ke neng lü	probability of death
si wang lü	death rate; mortality rate
si wang yuan yin	cause of death
si wang zheng ming	death certificate
su zao yi qun*	synthetic cohort
suo you zhe	owner
tai ci	birth order
tai er si wang	fetal mortality
te zheng	characteristic; attribute
ting jing	menopause; climacteric
tong dui	cohort
tong dui sheng yu li	cohort fertility
tong hua	assimilation

*Translates the English but is not generally used.

Chinese (Pin-yin)	English
tong ju	cohabitation
tong qin*	commuting
tong qin zhe*	commuter
tu biao	diagram; graph
tuan ti	group
wai guo ren	alien, n.
wai yan fa	extrapolation
wai yi	emigration
wai yin di	exogenous (of deaths)
wan quan sheng yu li	completed fertility
wan zheng sheng ming biao	complete life table
wei chan si wang	perinatal mortality
wei hun	never married
wei xian lü	risk
wei zhang ju min	squatter
wen ding ren kou	stable population
wu da	nonresponse
wu nong ren kou	farm population
wu ye	unemployed, adj.
wu ye zhe	unemployed person
xian zhu du	level of significance
xian zhu ren kou	de facto population; enumerated population
xiang cun	village
xiao cun	hamlet
xiao xue jiao yu	primary education
xin sheng er si wang	neonatal mortality
xin sheng ying er si wang lü	post-neonatal mortality
xing bi li	sex ratio
xing bie	sex
xing jiao	coitus; sexual intercourse
xing jiao hou bi yun wan	postcoital contraceptive
xing jiao zhong zhi	coitus interruptus; withdrawal

*Translates the English but is not generally used.

Chinese (Pin-yin)	English
xing nian bie bi lü	sex-age-specific rate
xuan yang	sampling
xuan yang wu cha	sampling error
yang ben	sample, n.
yang ben diao cha	sample survey
yi chu	departure (of emigrants)
yi chuan	heredity
yi chuan xue	genetics
yi hun fu nü	married woman
yi hun nan ren	married man
yi lai bi	dependency ratio
yi min	migrant
yi qun	cohort
yi ru	immigration
yi zhi ren	displaced person
yin bie si wang lü	cause-specific mortality rate
yin er si wang	infant mortality
yin da zhe	respondent (census)
ying hai	infant; baby
you mu	nomad
you sheng xue	eugenics
yuan shi zi liao	primary data
yue jing	menstruation
zai hun	remarriage
zao chan	premature birth; prematurity (of births)
zhang ding di	provisional
zhen	town
zheng qun chou yang	cluster sampling
zheng shu	round number
zhi biao	indicator
zhi jie fa biao zhun hua	direct method of standardization
zhi shu	index
zhi ye	occupation
zhong sheng yu lü	total fertility rate

Chinese (Pin-yin)	English
zhong wei di	median, adj.
zhong wei shu	median, n.
zhong xin du shi	central city
zhong xue jiao yu	secondary education
zhong zu	race, n.
zhou qi fa	rhythm method; periodic abstinence
zhu zhai	dwelling unit; residence
zhui zong	follow-up, n.
zhun que	accuracy
zhun wen ding ren kou	quasi-stable population
zi gong	uterus; womb
zi gong mao	diaphragm; pessary
zi gong nei bi yun qi	intra-uterine device; IUD
zi liao	data
zi ran duo tai	spontaneous abortion; miscarriage
zi ran qu	natural area
zi ran zeng jia	natural increase
zi wo cha ji	self-enumeration
zi you jie he	free union
zong	gross
zong jiao	religion
zu	set, n.
zu hu	tenant
zu ji	national origin

Chinese (Wade-Giles) to English

Chinese (Wade-Giles)	English
ch'a-chi	enumeration
ch'a-chi p'ien-ti	underenumeration
ch'a-chi yüan	enumerator
ch'a-i	difference
ch'a-pieh szu-wang	differential mortality
ch'an-fu szu-wang	maternal mortality; puerperal mortality
chan-ting-ti	provisional
ch'ang-chu jen k'ou	de jure population; resident population
chen	town
ch'en hou wan	morning-after pill
ch'eng-chen	urban
cheng-ch'ün ch'ou-yang	cluster sampling
ch'eng-jen	adult, n.
ch'eng-shih	city
cheng-shu	round number
chi-chi-hsing yi-chih	positive check
chi-chü-chê	boarder; lodger
chi-chun	base, n.
chi-ho p'ing-chün shu	geometric mean
chi-hui	chance
chi-pen tzu-liao	basic data
chi-ping	disease; morbidity
chi-shu (sheng-ming piao)	radix (of a life table)
chi-t'i hsüan-yang	cluster sampling
chi-yü yang-pen	probability sample
chia-ch'üang p'ing-chün shu	weighted mean; weighted average
chia-t'ing	family
chia-t'ing chi-hua	family planning
chia-t'ing chin-t'ieh	family allowance; family subsidy
chia-t'ing pu-chu	family subsidy; family allowance
chia-t'ing ta-hsiao	family size
ch'iang-p'o ch'ien-i	forced migration
chiao cheng-ti	revised; corrected
chiao hu lieh piao	cross-tabulation
chiao-p'ai	(religious) denomination
chieh-ho	union

Chinese (Wade-Giles)	English
chieh-hun	marriage
chieh-hun chiu-tu	duration of marriage
chieh-hun lü	marriage rate
chieh-kuo hun	ever married, adj.
chien-chieh fa piao-chun hua	indirect method of standardization
ch'ien-i	migration
chien-ke	spacing (of births), n.
chien-yao sheng-ming piao	abridged lfe table
chih-chieh fa piao-chun hua	direct method of standardization
chih-piao	indicator
chih-shu	index
chih-yeh	occupation
ch'in-shu	relatives; kin
ching-ch'i	menstrual cycle
ching-chi ch'eng-chang	economic growth
ching-chi fa-chan	economic development
ching-chi pu-men	sector of the economy
ching ch'ien-i	net migration
ching-chih jen-k'ou	stationary population
ch'ing-ch'un ch'i	puberty
ching-hsi shu-tzu	refined figure
ch'ing k'uang pu-ming wu ta	unknown; not stated
ch'ing-nien ch'i	adolescence
ch'ing shao nien	adolescent
ching tsai sheng ch'an lü	net reproduction rate
ching-tzu	sperm
ch'ing-yüan chieh-ho	consensual union
chiu-yeh	employed
chou-ch'i fa	rhythm method; periodic abstinence
ch'ou-yang	sampling, n.
chu-chai	dwelling unit; residence
ch'u-ch'ao	menarche
chü-chu jen-k'ou	resident population; de jure population
chü-min	inhabitant
ch'u-sheng lü	birth rate

Chinese (Wade-Giles)	English
ch'u-sheng sheng-ming yü-ch'i-chih	life expectancy at birth
ch'ü-shih	trend
ch'ü-yü	region; territory; area
ch'üan chü	range
ch'üan-shu	(statistical) weight
chüan-shu	dependent, n.
chüan-shu tzu-nü	dependent children
chüeh-yü	sterilization
chui-tsung	follow-up, n.
ch'un	net
ch'ün-chi	heaping; bunching
chun-ch'üeh	accuracy
chun wen-ting jen-k'ou	quasi-stable population
chün-yün hua	smoothing (of a curve)
chung hsin tu shih	central city
chung-hsüeh chiao-yü	secondary education
chung-tsu	race, n.
chung-wei shu	median, n.
chung-wei-ti	median, adj.
fa-ping lü	incidence rate
fa-tsê	code, v.
fan-chih	reproduction
fang-chih hsing yi-chih	preventive check
fang-shih	mode
fang-wen piao	schedule, n.
fang-wen yüan	interviewer
fen-hsi	analysis
fen-lei	classify
fen-pu	(frequency) distribution
fen-ts'eng hsüan-yang	stratified sampling
feng-pi jen-k'ou	closed population
fu-fu	(married) couple
fu-mu	parents
fu-mu shen-fen	parenthood
fu-nü	female, n.; woman

228

Chinese (Wade-Giles)	English
fu-sê	(skin) color
fu-shu ch'eng-chang	negative growth
hai fu pi	child-woman ratio
hai-mien	(contraceptive) sponge
han-hua	acculturation
ho-fa	legitimacy
ho-fa-ti	legitimate
ho-hsin chia-t'ing	nuclear family
hou-tai	offspring; progeny
hsiang-ts'un	village
hsiao-hsüeh chiao-yü	primary education
hsiao-ts'un	hamlet
hsien-chu jen-k'ou	de facto population; enumerated population
hsien-chu tu	level of significance
hsin-sheng-erh szu-wang	neonatal mortality
hsin-sheng ying-erh szu-wang lü	post-neonatal mortality
hsing-chiao	coitus; sexual intercourse
hsing-chiao chung-chih	coitus interruptus; withdrawal
hsing-chaio hou pi-yün wan	postcoital contraceptive
hsing nien pieh pi-lü	sex-age-specific rate
hsing pi li	sex ratio
hsing-pieh	sex
hsüan-yang	sampling, n.
hsüan-yang wu-ch'a	sampling error
hu-chang	head of a household
hu-chu	head of a household
hu-k'ou	household
hu-yüan	member of a household
huai-yün	conception; pregnancy; gestation
hui-kui ch'ien-i	return migration; remigration
hun-yin	nuptiality
hun-yin chuang-k'uang	marital status; civil status; conjugal status
huo-sheng yü	live birth
i-chih jen	displaced person

Chinese (Wade-Giles)	English
i-ch'u	departure (of emigrants)
i-ch'uan	heredity
i-ch'uan hsüeh	genetics
i-hun fu-nü	married woman
i-hun nan-jen	married man
i-ju	immigration
i-min	migrant
jen	person
jen-k'ou	population
jen-k'ou cheng-ts'ê	population policy
jen-k'ou chien-ti	depopulation; population decline
jen-k'ou chin-tzu t'a	population pyramid
jen-k'ou ke-ming	demographic transition
jen-k'ou mi-tu	population density
jen-k'ou p'ien-ti	underpopulation
jen-k'ou pien-keng	demographic transition
jen-k'ou teng-chi	population register
jen-k'ou tseng-chang	population growth
jen-k'ou t'ung-chi	population statistics
jen-k'ou t'ung-chi hsüeh	demography
jen-k'ou t'ung-chi hsüeh-chê	demographer
jen-k'ou ya-li	population pressure
jen-k'ou yü-ts'ê	population forecast; population projection
jen-kung to t'ai	induced abortion
jen-shen	gestation; pregnancy
jen-wen shang-t'ai	human ecology
k'ai-fang jen-k'ou	open population
kao ling	senility
kao-teng chiao-yü	higher education
ko-jen	individual
ko-li	segregation
k'o-neng lü	probability
k'o-yü-ti (t'ai-erh)	viable (of a fetus)
k'ou-fu pi-yün yao	oral contraceptive
ku-chi	estimate, n. and v.; estimation

Chinese (Wade-Giles)	English
ku yu lü	intrinsic rate; true rate
kuan-hsi	relationship (to head of a household)
kui-hua	naturalization
kui-lei chi	(machine) sorter
kung-kung wei-sheng	public health
kung-min	citizen
kung-yeh	industry
kuo-chi	nationality
kuo-chi chi'ien-i	international migration
kuo-chia	country; nation; state
kuo-jen	people (nation)
kuo-k'o	transient, n.
kuo-nei ch'ien-i	internal migration
kuo-sheng jen-k'ou	overpopulation
kuo-wai sheng	foreign-born
lao ch'u-nü	spinster
lao-hua	aging, n.
lao-nien	old age
lao-nien hsüeh	gerontology
lao-nien ping-hsüeh	geriatrics
lao-tung jen-k'ou	economically active population
li-hun	divorce
lieh piao	tabulate
liu-hsing lü	prevalence rate
liu-hsing ping	epidemic, n.
liu-lang-chê	vagrant; person of no fixed abode
lü	rate
luan-tzu	ovum
min-tsu	ethnic group
mo-hsing	model, n.
mo-ni	simulation
mu-yü	mother tongue; native language
nan	male, n.; man
nan-min	refugee
nei-ch'a fa	interpolation

Chinese (Wade-Giles)	English
nei-fa-ti	endogenous (of deaths)
nien-ch'ing hua	younging (of a population)
nien-ling	age
nien-ling chieh-kou	age structure; age distribution
nien-ling fen-pu	age distribution; age structure
nien-ling tsu	age group(ing)
nien-ling ts'ung*	age group(ing); age bracket
nien-pieh lü	age-specific rate
nung-ts'un	rural
nung-yeh jen-k'ou	agricultural population
pai-fen chih . . .	. . . percent
pai-fen pi	percentage
p'ai-luan	ovulation
pao-hsien t'ao	condom; sheath
p'ei-ou	spouse
p'ei-t'ai	fetus
pei tiao-ch'a te tui-hsiang	subject, n.
pen-kuo-sheng	native-born
pi-li	proportion; ratio
pi-yün	contraception
pi-yün fa	contraceptive method
pi-yün kung-chü	contraceptive, n. (barrier)
pi-yün wan-yao	contraceptive pill
pi-yün yao-wu	contraceptive, n. (pill)
piao	table, n.
piao-chun hua	standardized (of a rate)
piao-chun jen-k'ou	standard population
piao-chun p'ien-ch'a	standard deviation
piao-chun tu-hui ch'ü	standard metropolitan area; agglomeration; conurbation
piao-chun wu-ch'a	standard error
piao-shi	form, n.
pien i	variation; variability
pien-shu	variable, n.

*Translates the English but is not generally used.

232

Chinese (Wade-Giles)	English
p'ing chü	concubinage
p'ing-chün jen-k'ou	mean population
p'ing-chün shu	mean, n.; average, n.
p'ing-chün-ti	mean, adj.; average, adj.
p'ing-chün-ti ch'a-shu	mean deviation
po-tung	fluctuation
p'u-ch'a	census
p'u-ch'a ch'ü	census tract
pu-jen	sterility; infecundity
pu-ju-ch'i (yen-ch'ang)	lactation (prolonged)
san-pu	dispersion; scatter, n.
shao-shu min-tsu	minority
shê-hui chieh-chi	social class
shê-hui chieh-ts'eng	social stratification
shê-hui ching-chi t'uan-t'i	socio-economic group
shê-hui liu-tung	social mobility
sheng-ch'an li	productive forces
sheng-ch'an neng li sheng-ch'an lü	productivity
sheng chi tu	subsistence level
sheng-chih li	fecundability; fecundity
sheng-hsü	parity
sheng-huo ch'eng-tu	standard of living
sheng-huo shui-p'ing	level of living
sheng-ming chung-wei tu	median length of life
sheng-ming fu-tu	life span
sheng-ming k'o-neng ch'ang-tu	probable length of life
sheng-ming piao	life table; mortality table
sheng-ming p'ing-chün-tu	mean length of life
sheng-ming t'ung-chi	vital statistics
sheng-ming yü-ch'i-chih	life expectancy; expectation of life
sheng-ts'un tsung nien shu	total years lived
sheng tzu-liao	raw data
sheng-yü	birth
sheng-yü chieh-chih	birth control
sheng-yü chien-ko	birth interval
sheng-yü li	fertility; natality

Chinese (Wade-Giles)	English
sheng-yü lü	fertility rate
shih-chiao	suburb
shih-chien shu-lieh	time series
shih-tai	generation
shih-tai ch'ang-tu	length of a generation
shih-tu jen-k'ou	population optimum; optimum population
shih-tzu-chê	literate person
shou-ming	longevity; length of life
shou-t'ai	fertilization
shou-tsu	siblings
shou-tu	capital (city)
shu-ching-kuan ch'ieh-ch'u-shu	vasectomy
shu-lieh	series
shu-lüan-kuan chieh-cha	tubal ligation
shu-lüan-kuan ch'ieh-ch'u-shu	salpingectomy
shu-mu	count, n.; number, n.
shu-tzu, t'u piao	figure, n.
shuai-lao	senility
so-yu-chê	owner
su-tsao yi-ch'ün*	synthetic cohort
szu-ch'an	stillbirth
szu-sheng	illegitimacy
szu-sheng-ti	illegitimate
szu-sheng-tzu	illegitmate child
szu-wang	death; mortality
szu-wang cheng-ming	death certificate
szu-wang k'o-neng lü	probability of death
szu-wang lü	death rate; mortality rate
szu-wang yüan-yin	cause of death
ta k'a	punch card
ta-k'ung	punch, n.
t'ai-erh szu wang	fetal mortality
tai-piao yang-pen	representative sample

*Translates the English but is not generally used.

Chinese (Wade-Giles)	English
t'ai-tz'u	birth order
tan shen	single
tao-ta	arrival (of immigrants)
tao-tê chieh-chih	moral restraint
t'e-cheng	characteristic; attribute
teng-chi	registration
teng-chi kuo-ti	underregistration
ti-chu	landlord
ti-ch'ü	area; territory; region
ti-ch'ü hsüan-yang	area sampling
ti-li fen-pu	geographical distribution; spatial distribution
ti-li i-tung	geographical mobility; spatial mobility
ti-tuan	block, n.
ti-yü	territory; area; region
tiao-ch'a	survey, n.
tiao-ch'a piao	questionnaire, schedule, n.
tien-hsing	model, n.
tien-nao	(electronic) computer
t'ing ching	menopause; climacteric
to-sheng yü	multiple birth
to-shu-te	modal
to t'ai	abortion
tsai-hun	remarriage
ts'an-fei	disability
tsao-ch'an	premature birth; prematurity (of births)
tsu	set, n.
ts'u (lü)	crude (of a rate)
tsu-chi	national origin
tsu-hu	tenant
tsu tsai sheng ch'an lü	gross reproduction rate
ts'u tzu liao	primary data
ts'un-huo che	survivor
ts'un-huo kai-lü	probability of survival
tsung	gross
tsung-chiao	religion

Chinese (Wade-Giles)	English
tsung sheng-yü lü	total fertility rate
t'u piao	diagram; graph
tu-shen	bachelor
tu-shen sheng-huo	celibacy
tu-shih hua	urbanization
t'uan-t'i	group
tui-chi	heaping; bunching
t'ung-chin*	commuting
t'ung-chin-chê*	commuter
t'ung-chü	cohabitation
t'ung-hua	assimilation
t'ung-tui	cohort
t'ung-tui sheng-yü li	cohort fertility
tzu-jan ch'ü	natural area
tzu-jan to t'ai	spontaneous abortion; miscarriage
tzu-jan tseng-chia	natural increase
tz'u jen-k'ou	subpopulation
tz'u k'ai-fa kuo-chia	less developed country; underdeveloped country
tzu-kung	uterus; womb
tzu-kung mao	diaphragm; pessary
tzu-kung nei pi-yün-ch'i	intra-uterine device; IUD
tzu-liao	data
tzu-wo ch'a-chi	self-enumeration
tz'u yang-pen	subsample
tzu-yu chieh-ho	free union
wai-i	emigration
wai-kuo jen	alien, n.
wai yen fa	extrapolation
wai-yin-ti	exogenous (of a death)
wan-cheng sheng-min piao	complete life table
wan-ch'üan sheng-yü li	completed fertility
wei-ch'an szu-wang	perinatal mortality

*Translates the English but is not generally used.

Chinese (Wade-Giles)	English
wei-chang chü-min	squatter
wei-hsien lü	risk
wei hun	never married
wen-ting jen k'ou	stable population
wu-nung jen-k'ou	farm population
wu ta	nonresponse
wu-yeh	unemployed, adj.
wu-yeh-chê	unemployed person
yang-pen	sample, n.
yang-pen tiao-ch'a	sample survey
yi-ch'ün	cohort
yi-lai pi	dependency ratio
yin-pieh szu-wang lü	causes-specific mortality rate
ying-erh szu wang	infant mortality
ying-hai	infant; baby
ying-ta-chê	respondent (census)
yu-mu	nomad
yu-sheng hsüeh	eugenics
yüan-shih tzu-liao	primary data
yüeh-ching	menstruation

Russian–English

Russian	English
abort	abortion
abort, iskusstvennyi	induced abortion
abort, neprednamerennyi	spontaneous abortion
abort, neproizvol'nyi	miscarriage; spontaneous abortion
akkumuliatsiia	heaping; bunching; accumulation
analiz	analysis
anketa	questionnaire
areal	natural area
assimilatsiia	assimilation
baza	base, n.
beremennost'	pregnancy; gestation
beremennosti, dlitel'nost'	gestation
besplodie	infecundity; sterility
bezbrachie	celibacy
bezhenets	refugee
bezrabotnye	unemployed, n.
bezrabotnyi	unemployed, adj.
biologicheskii ritm	rhythm method
bol'nykh, protsent	prevalence rate
brachnost'	nuptiality
brachnosti, koeffitsient	marriage rate
brachnyi soiuz	union
brak	marriage
brak, fakticheskii	free union
brak, grazhdanskii	consensual union
brak, povtornyi	remarriage
brak, vstuplenie v novyi	remarriage
braka, prodolzhitel'nost'	duration of marriage
brake, litsa, kogda-libo sostoiavshie v,	ever married
brake, ne sostoiashchii v,	bachelor
brake, nikogda ne sostoiavshie v,	never married
brutto	gross
brutto-koeffitsient vosproizvodstva	gross reproduction rate

Russian	English
chastoty (zabolevanii), koeffitsient	incidence rate
chelovek	man; individual
cheloveko-let, summa	total years lived
chislo	number, n.; figure, n.
chislo detei	parity; birth order
chislo, okruglennoe	round number
chlen domokhoziaistva	member of a household
dannye, neobrabotannye	raw data
dannye o estestvennom dvizhenii naseleniia	vital statistics
dannye, obrabotannye	refined data
dannye, obshchie	crude data
dannye, osnovnye	basic data
dannye, pervichnye	primary data
dannye, statisticheskie	data
demograf	demographer
demograficheskaia politika	population policy
demograficheskaia revoliutsiia	demographic transition; demographic revolution; vital revolution
demograficheskaia statistika	population statistics
demograficheskii perekhod	demographic transition; demographic revolution
demograficheskoe davlenie	population pressure
demografiia	demography
depopuliatsiia	depopulation
detei, chislo	parity
deti, nakhodiashchiesia na izhdivenii	dependent children
detnost'	child-woman ratio
detorozhdeniia, regulirovanie	birth control
detskaia smertnost'	infant mortality
detskaia smertnost' na pervom godu zhizni v vozraste starshe odnogo mesiatsa	post-neonatal mortality
detskaia smertnost', ranniaia	neonatal mortality
devitsa	spinster
devushka	female adolescent, n.
diafragma	diaphragm

Russian	English
diagramma	diagram
dinamika	trend
dispersiia	dispersion; scatter, n.
dlina pokoleniia	length of a generation
dlitel'nost' beremennosti	gestation; pregnancy
domokhoziaistva, chlen	member of a household
domokhoziaistvo	household
dostovernost'	accuracy
dozhitiia, veroiatnost'	probability of survival
dozhivaiushchii	survivor
dusha	soul
dvor	household
ekologiia cheloveka	human ecology
ekonomicheskoe razvitie	economic development; economic growth
ekstrapoliatsiia	extrapolation
ekzogennaia (smertnost')	exogenous (of a death)
elektronno-vychislitel'naia mashina	computer (electronic)
emigratsiia	emigration
endogennaia (smertnost')	endogenous (of a death)
epidemiia	epidemic, n.
estestvennyi prirost	natural increase
etnicheskaia gruppa	ethnic group
evgenika	eugenics
EVM (elektronnaia vychislitel'naia mashina)	computer (electronic)
fakticheskii brak	free union
fakticheskoe naselenie	de facto population
fetus	fetus
fluktuatsiia	fluctuation
forma	form, n.; mode
genetika	genetics
geograficheskaia mobil'nost'	geographical mobility
geriatriia	geriatrics
gerontologiia	gerontology
gorod	city

Russian	English
gorod, tsentral'nyi	central city
gorodok	town
gorodskaia aglomeratsiia	agglomeration; standard metropolitan area
gorodskoe	urban
gosudarstvo	state, n.
grafik	graph
gramotnyi chelovek	literate person
grazhdanin	citizen
grazhdanskii brak	consensual union
gruppa	group
gruppovaia vyborka	cluster sampling
iaitso	ovum
iazyk, rodnoi	mother tongue; native language
imeiushchii rabotu	employed
immigratsiia	immigration
indeks	index
inostranets	alien, n.
intergeneticheskii interval	birth interval
interpoliatsiia	interpolation
interval mezhdu rozhdeniiami	birth interval
ischerpannaia plodovitost'	completed fertility
iskhodnaia sovokupnost' rodivshikhsia	radix (of a life table)
ispravlennyi	corrected
istinnyi koeffitsient	intrinsic rate
iunosha	male adolescent, n.
iunost'	adolescence
iuridicheskoe naselenie	de jure population
izhdivenets	dependent, n.
izmenenie klassovogo sostava	social mobility
kachestvennyi priznak	characteristic; attribute
kachestvo	characteristic; attribute
kalendarnyi metod	rhythm method
kharakteristika	characteristic; attribute
khoziain doma	landlord

Russian	English
khoziaistva, otrasl' (narodnogo)	sector of the economy
khutor	hamlet
klass, obshchestvennyi	social class
klassifitsirovat'	classify
klimaks	climacteric; menopause
kochevnik	nomad
kodirovat'	code, v.
kodu, shifrovat' po	code, v.
koeffitsient	rate, n.
koeffitsient brachnosti	marriage rate
koeffitsient chastoty (zabolevanii)	incidence rate
koeffitsient, istinnyi	intrinsic rate
koeffitsient plodovitosti	fertility rate
koeffitsient plodovitosti, summarnyi	total fertility rate
koeffitsient, povozrastnyi	age-specific rate
koeffitsient rozhdaemosti	birth rate
koeffitsient smertnosti	death rate
koeffitsient smertnosti ot opredelnnykh prichin	cause-specific mortality rate
koeffitsienty, polo-vozrastnye	sex-age-specific rate
kogorta	cohort
kogorta, sinteticheskaia	synthetic cohort
kogorty, plodovitost'	cohort fertility
koïtus	coitus
kolebanie	fluctuation
kolpachok	cervical cap; pessary
kontrol' rozhdaemosti	birth control
konurbatsiia	conurbation
kormlenie, udlinennoe grudnoe	lactation, prolonged
kosvennyi metod standartizatsii	indirect method of standardization
kvartal	block, n.
litsa, kogda-libo sostoiavshie v brake	person who is ever married
litso	person
litso muzhskogo pola	male, n.

Russian	English
litso, ne imeiushchee postoiannogo mestozhi- tel'stva	vagrant
litso, ne soobshchivshee svedenii	person who made a nonresponse
litso, sovershaiushchee reguliarnye poezdki	commuter
litso zhenskogo pola	female, n.
maiatnikovaia migratsiia	commuting
malorazvitaia strana	underdeveloped country
materinskaia smertnost'	maternal mortality; puerperal mortality
materinstvo	motherhood
matka	uterus; womb
mediana	median, n.
mediannyi	median, adj.
menarkhe	menarche
menopauza	menopause; climacteric
men'shinstvo	minority
menstrual'nyi tsikl	menstrual cycle
menstruatsiia	menstruation
mertvorozhdenie	stillbirth
mestnyi urozhenets	native-born
mestozhil'stva, litso, ne imeiushchee postoian- nogo	vagrant; person of no fixed abode
mestozhitel'stvo	residence
mezhdunarodnaia migratsiia	international migration
migrant	migrant
migratsiia	migration
migratsiia, maiatnikovaia	commuting
migratsiia, mezhdunarodnaia	international migration
migratsiia, netto-	net migration
migratsiia, obratnaia	return migration; remigration
migratsiia, prinuditel'naia	forced migration
migratsiia, vnutrenniaia	internal migration
mladenets	infant
mnogoplodnye rody	multiple birth
mobil'nost', geograficheskaia	geographical mobility

245

Russian	English
mobil'nost', sotsial'naia	social mobility
mobil'nost', territorial'naia	spatial mobility; geographical mobility
mod	mode
modal'nyi	modal
model'	model, n.
muzhchina	man
muzhskogo pola, litso	male, n.
nachal'noe obrazovanie	primary education
nanimatel' (zhilogo pomeshcheniia)	tenant
narod	people
naselenie	population
naselenie, fakticheskoe	de facto population
naselenie, iuridicheskoe	de jure population
naselenie, kvazi-stabil'noe	quasi-stable population
naselenie, nalichnoe	enumerated population
naselenie, otkrytoe	open population
naselenie, postoiannoe	resident population
naselenie, samodeiatel'noe	economically active population
naselenie, sel'skoe	rural population
naselenie, sel'skokhoziaistvennoe	agricultural population
naselenie, srednee	mean population
naselenie, stabilnoe	stable population
naselenie, standartnoe	standard population
naselenie, statsionarnoe	stationary population
naselenie, zakrytoe	closed population
naselenie, zamknutoe	closed population
naseleniia, nedouchet chislennosti	underenumeration
naseleniia, optimal'naia chislennost'	optimum population
naseleniia, optimum	population optimum
naseleniia, perspektivnoe ischislenie	population forecast
naseleniia, podgruppa	subpopulation
naseleniia, pokazatel' plotnosti	population density
naseleniia, prognoz	population projection
naseleniia, rost	population growth

Russian	English
naseleniia, spiski	population register
naseleniia, ubyl'	population decline
naselennost', nedostatochnaia	underpopulation
nasledstvennost'	heredity
natsiia	nation
natsional'noe proiskhozhdenie	national origin
natsional'nost'	nationality
naturalizatsiia	naturalization
ne sostoiashchii v brake	bachelor
ne ukazan	unknown
nedonoshennoe rozhdenie	premature birth
nedonoshennost'	prematurity (of births)
nedostatochnaia naselennost'	underpopulation
nedouchet chislennosti naseleniia	underenumeration
neobrabotannye dannye	raw data
neorganicheskaia (smertnost')	exogenous (of a death)
nepolnaia registratsiia	underregistration
netrudosposobnost'	disability
netto-	net
netto-koeffitsient vosproizvodstva	net reproduction rate
netto-migratsiia	net migration
nezakonnoe rozhdenie	illegitimacy
nezakonnorozhdennyi	illegitimate
nezakonnyi	illegitimate
nezaniatyi	unemployed, adj.
nezhenatyi	bachelor
nikogda ne sostoiavshie v brake	never-married
nomer rozhdeniia	birth order; parity
novorozhdennykh, smertnost'	neonatal mortality
nuklearnaia sem'ia	nuclear family
oblast' geograficheskogo rasprostraneniia	natural area
obrabotannye dannye	refined data
obratnaia migratsiia	return migration; remigration
obrazovanie, nachal'noe	primary education

247

Russian	English
obrazovanie, srednee	secondary education
obrazovanie, vysshee	higher education
obshchestvennyi klass	social class
obshchie dannye	crude data
obshchii (koeffitsient)	crude (of a rate)
obsledovanie	survey, n.
obsledovanie, vyborochnoe	sample survey
odinokie	single
okruglennoe chislo	round number
oplodotvorenie	fertilization
oprashivaemoe litso	(census) respondent
optimal'naia chislennost' naseleniia	optimum population; population optimum
optimum naseleniia	optimum population; population optimum
organicheskaia (smertnost)	endogenous (of a death)
oshibka, standartnaia	standard error
oshibka vyborki	sampling error
osnovnye dannye	basic data
ot'ezd	departure (of emigrants)
otklonenie, srednee	mean deviation
otklonenie, srednekvadraticheskoe	standard deviation
otnoshenie	ratio
otnoshenie chisla detei k chislu materei	child-woman ratio
otnoshenie chisla izhdiventsev k chislu rabo-taiushchikh	dependency ratio
otnoshenie (k glave sem'i)	relationship (to head of household)
otrasl' (narodnogo) khoziaistva	sector of the economy
otritsatel'nyi prirost	negative growth
otsenivat'	estimate, v.
otsenka	estimate, n.; estimation
ottsovstvo	fatherhood
ovuliatsiia	ovulation
para (supruzheskaia)	(married) couple
perechislenie	enumeration
perekhod, demograficheskii	demographic transition; demographic revolution

Russian	English
peremennaia	variable, n.
peremeshchennoe litso	displaced person
perenaselenie	overpopulation
perepis'	census
perepisnoi list	schedule, n.
perepisnoi raion	census tract
peresmotrennyi	revised
pereviazyvanie matochnykh pridatkov	salpingectomy
pereviazyvanie matochnykh trub	tubal ligation
perforatsiia	punch, n.
perforatsionnaia kartochka	punch card
perinatal'naia smertnost'	perinatal mortality
periodicheskoe vozderzhanie	periodic abstinence
perspektivnoe ischislenie naseleniia	population forecast
pervichnye dannye	primary data
plod, utrobnyi	fetus
plodovitost'	fertility
plodovitost', ischerpannaia	completed fertility
plodovitost' kogorty	cohort fertility
plodovitost', potentsial'naia	fecundity
plodovitosti, koeffitsient	fertility rate
plodovitosti, summarnyi koeffitsient	total fertility rate
ploshchad'	area
poddannyi	subject, n.
podgruppa naseleniia	subpopulation
podschet	count, n.
podvyborka	subsample
pokazatel'	indicator
pokazatel' plotnosti naseleniia	population density
pokolenie	generation
pokoleniia, dlina	length of a generation
pol	sex
polnye tablitsy smertnosti	completed life table
polo-vozrastnye koeffitsienty	sex-age-specific rate

Russian	English
polov, sootnoshenie	sex ratio
polovaia zrelost'	puberty
polovoe snoshenie	sexual intercourse
polozhitel'naia proverka	positive check
pol'zovanie protivozachatochnymi sredstvami	contraception
poriadok rodov	birth order; parity
posobie sem'iam	family allowance; family subsidy
potentsial'naia plodovitost'	fecundity
potomstvo	offspring; progeny
povozrastnyi koeffitsient	age-specific rate
povtornaia rassylka perepisnykh listov	follow-up, n.
povtornyi brak	remarriage
predupreditel'nye mery	moral restraint; preventive check
preduprezhdeniia zachatiia, sposob	contraceptive method
predvaritel'nyi	provisional
prervannoe snoshenie	coitus interruptus; withdrawal
preventivnaia proverka	preventive check; moral restraint
prezervativ	condom
priamoi metod standartizatsii	direct method of standardization
pribytie	arrival (of immigrants)
prichina smerti	cause of death
prigorod	suburb
prinuditel'naia migratsiia	forced migration
priobschenie k kul'ture	acculturation
prirost, estestvennyi	natural increase
prirost, otritsatel'nyi	negative growth; population decline
prodolzhitel'nost' braka	duration of marriage
prodolzhitel'nost' zhizni pri rozhdenii, sred- niaia	life expectancy at birth
prodolzhitel'nost', sredniaia	life expectancy
prodolzhitel'nost' predstoiashchei zhizni, ve- roiatnaia	probable length of life
prodolzhitel'nost' zhizni	longevity; length of life
prodolzhitel'nost' zhizni, sredniaia	mean length of life

Russian	English
professiia	occupation
prognoz naseleniia	population projection
proizvoditel'nost'	productivity
promyshlennost'	industry
proportsiia	proportion
protivozachatochnoe sredstvo	contraceptive, n.
protivozachatochnymi sredstvami, pol'zovanie	contraception
protivozachatochnye sredstva dlia vnutrennego priema	oral contraceptive
protivozachatochnye sredstva, prinimaemye posle snosheniia	postcoital contraceptive
protivozachatochnye tabletki	contraceptive pill
protsent	percentage; percent
protsent bol'nykh	prevalence rate
prozhitochnyi minimum	subsistence level
prozhitye gody zhizni	life span
rabotu, imeiushchii	employed
raion	region
raion, perepisnoi	census tract
ranniaia detskaia smertnost'	neonatal mortality
rasa	race, n.
raspisanie	schedule, n.
raspredelenie	(frequency) distribution
raspredelenie, territorial'noe	geographical distribution; spatial distribution
razlichie	difference
razlichiia v smertnosti	differential mortality
razmakh	range
razmerov sem'i, regulirovanie	family planning
razmery sem'i	family size
razvitie, ekonomicheskoe	economic development; economic growth
razvivaiushchaiasia strana	less developed country; underdeveloped country
razvod	divorce
rebenok	baby
region	region

Russian	English
registrator	enumerator
registratsiia	registration
registratsiia, nepolnaia	underregistration
regulirovanie detorozhdeniia	birth control
regulirovanie intervalov mezhdu rozhdeniiami	spacing (of births)
regulirovanie razmerov sem'i	family planning
religiia	religion
reprezentativnaia vyborka	representative sample
revolutsiia, demograficheskaia	demographic revolution; demographic transition
riad	set, n.
riad, dinamicheskii	time series
riad, vremennyi	time series
risk	risk
rod	kin; relatives
roditeli	parents
rodivshiisia v drugoi strane	foreign-born
rodnoi iazyk	mother tongue; native language
rodnye (brat'ia i sestry)	siblings
rodov, poriadok	birth order; parity
rodstvenniki	relatives; kin
rody, mnogoplodnye	multiple birth
rost naseleniia	population growth
rozhdaemost'	natality
rozhdaemosti, koeffitsient	birth rate
rozhdaemosti, kontrol'	birth control
rozhdenie	birth
rozhdenie, nedonoshennoe	premature birth
rozhdenie, nezakonnoe	illegitimacy
rozhdeniia, nomer	birth order; parity
rozhdeniiami, regulirovanie intervalov mezhdu	spacing (of births)
samoischislenie	self-enumeration
schet	count, n.
schetchik	enumerator; interviewer

Russian	English
segregatsiia	segregation
selo	village
sel'skoe	rural
sel'skoe naselenie	rural population
sel'skokhoziaistvennoe naselenie	agricultural population
semeinoe polozhenie	marital status; civil status; conjugal status
semi'i, razmery	family size
sem'i, regulirovanie razmerov	family planning
sem'ia	family
sem'ia, nuklearnaia	nuclear family
sem'iam, posobie	family allowance; family subsidy
senil'nost'	senility
seriia	series
shifrovat' po kodu	code, v.
simuliatsiia	simulation
skvatter	squatter
smert'	death
smerti, prichina	cause of death
smerti, svidetel'stvo o	death certificate
smerti, veroiatnost'	probability of death
smertnost'	mortality
smertnost', detskaia	infant mortality
smertnost', detskaia, na pervom godu zhizni v vozraste starshe odnogo mesiatsa	post-neonatal mortality
smertnost', materinskaia	maternal mortality; puerperal mortality
smertnost' novorozhdennykh	neonatal mortality
smertnost', perinatal'naia	perinatal mortality
smertnost', ranniaia detskaia	neonatal mortality
smertnost', vnutriutrobnaia	fetal mortality
smertnosti, koeffitsient	death rate
smertnosti, koeffitsient, ot opredelennykh prichin	cause-specific mortality rate
smertnosti, polnye tablitsy	complete life table
smertnosti, razlichiia v	differential mortality

Russian	English
smertnosti, sokrashchennye tablitsy	abridged life table
smertnosti, tablitsy	life table; mortality table
snoshenie, polovoe	sexual intercourse; coitus
snoshenie, prervannoe	coitus interruptus; withdrawal
sokrashchennye tablitsy smertnosti	abridged life table
sootnoshenie polov	sex ratio
sortirovshchik	(machine) sorter
sotsial'naia mobil'nost'	social mobility
sotsial'naia stratifikatsiia	social stratification
sotsial'no-ekonomicheskaia gruppa	socio-economic group
sovershaiushchee reguliarnye poezdki, litso	commuter
sozhitel'stvo	cohabitation
sozhitel'stvo, vnebrachnoe	concubinage
sperma	sperm
spiski naseleniia	population register
sposob preduprezhdeniia zachatiia	contraceptive method
sposobnost' k zachatiiu	fecundability
srednee chislo cheloveko-let, prozhitykh is-khodnoi massoi	median length of life
srednee naselenie	mean population
srednee obrazovanie	secondary education
srednee otklonenie	mean deviation
srednekvadraticheskoe otklonenie	standard deviation
sredniaia geometricheskaia	geometric mean
sredniaia prodolzhitel'nost' predstoiashchei zhizni	life expectancy; expectation of life
sredniaia prodolzhitel'nost' zhizni pri rozhdenii	life expectancy at birth
sredniaia prodolzhitel'nost' zhizni	mean length of life
sredniaia velichina	mean, n.; average, n.
srednii	mean, adj.; average, adj.
standartizatsii, kosvennyi metod	indirect method of standardization
standartizatsii, priamoi metod	direct method of standardization
standartizovannyi	standardized (of a rate)
standartnaia oshibka	standard error
starenie	aging, n.

Russian	English
starost'	old age
statisticheskie dannye	data
statistika, demograficheskaia	population statistics
sterilizatsiia	sterilization
steril'nost'	sterility
stolitsa	capital (city)
strana	country
strana, malorazvitaia	underdeveloped country
strana, razvivaiushchaiasia	less developed country; underdeveloped country
stratifikatsiia, sotsial'naia	social stratification
struktura	schedule, n.
summa cheloveko-let	total years lived
summarnyi koeffitsient plodovitosti	total fertility rate
suprug	spouse, m.
supruga	spouse, f.
svidetel'stvo o smerti	death certificate
svoistvo	attribute, characteristic
tablitsa	table, n.
tablitsy, kombinatsionnye	cross-tabulation
tablitsy smertnosti	life table; mortality table
tablitsy smertnosti, polnye	complete life table
tablitsy smertnosti, sokrashchennye	abridged life table
tabulirovat'	tabulate
tampon	(contraceptive) sponge
tendentsiia	trend
territorial'naia mobilnost'	spatial mobility; geographical mobility
territorial'noe raspredelenie	geographical distribution; spatial distribution
territorial'nyi vybor	area sampling
territoriia	territory
tipologicheskii vybor	stratified sampling
tsentral'nyi gorod	central city
tsvet	(skin) color
ubyl' naseleniia	population decline
uchet	count, n.; enumeration

Russian	English
urbanizatsiia	urbanization
uroven', zhiznennyi	standard of living
uroven' zhizni	level of living
uroven' znachimosti	level of significance
urozhenets, mestnyi	native-born
uslovnyi statisticheskii raion bol'shogo goroda s prigorodami	standard metropolitan area
utrobnyi plod	fetus
variatsiia	variation; variability
vasektomiia	vasectomy
vera	religion
veroiatnaia prodolzhitel'nost' predstoiashchei zhizni	probable length of life
veroiatnost'	probability
veroiatnost' dozhitiia	probability of survival
veroiatnost' smerti	probability of death
veroiatnostnaia (vzveshennaia) vyborka	probability sample
veroispovedanie	(religious) denomination
ves	(statistical) weight
vladelets	owner; landlord
vnebrachnoe sozhitel'stvo	concubinage
vnutrenniaia migratsiia	internal migration
vnutrimatochnye protivozachatochnye sredstva	intra-uterine device; IUD
vnutriutrobnaia smertnost'	fetal mortality
voprosnik	questionnaire
voprosy, ostavlennie bez otveta	not stated
vosproizvodstva, brutto-koeffitsient	gross reproduction rate
vosproizvodstva, netto-koeffitsient	net reproduction rate
vosproizvodstvo	reproduction
vozderzhanie, periodicheskoe	periodic abstinence
vozmozhnost'	risk; chance
vozrast	age
vozrastnaia gruppa	age group
vozrastnaia gruppirovka	age group
vozrastnaia struktura naseleniia	age structure

Russian	English
vozrastno-polovaia piramida	population pyramid
vozrastnoi sostav	age distribution
vremennaia utrata trudosposobnosti	disability
vremenno prozhivaiushchii	transient, n.
vstuplenie v novyi brak	remarriage
vybor, territorial'nyi	area sampling
vybor, tipologicheskii	stratified sampling
vyborka	sample, n.
vyborka, gruppovaia	cluster sampling
vyborka, reprezentativnaia	representative sample
vyborka, veroiatnostnaia (vzveshennaia)	probability sample
vyborki, oshibka	sampling error
vyborochnoe obsledovanie	sample survey
vyborochnyi metod	sampling, n.
vychislitel'naia mashina (elektronnaia)	(electronic) computer
vykidysh	miscarriage
vyravnivanie	smoothing (of a curve)
vyselki	hamlet
vysshee obrazovanie	higher education
vzroslyi	adult, n.
vzveshennaia seredina	weighted mean
zabolevaemost'	morbidity
zabolevanie	disease
zachatie	conception
zachatiiu, sposobnost' k	fecundability
zakonnorozhdennyi	legitimate
zakonnost'	legitimacy
zamuzhniaia zhenshchina	married woman
zaniatie	occupation
zaniatyi	employed
zdravookhranenie	public health
zhenatyi chelovek	married man
zhenshchina	woman
zhenskogo pola, litso	female, n.

Russian	English
zhilets	lodger
zhilishche	dwelling unit
zhitel'	inhabitant
zhivorozhdenie	live birth
zhivushchii v pansione	boarder
zhiznennyi uroven'	standard of living
zhiznesposobnyi	viable (of a fetus)
zhizni, prodolzhitel'nost'	longevity; length of life
zhizni, prozhitye gody	life span
zhizni, uroven'	level of living
zhizni, veroiatnaia prodolzhitel'nost' pred-stoiashchei	probable length of life
znachimosti, uroven'	level of significance

Collaborators

The following persons collaborated on the multilingual glossary:

French   Renee Petersen

Spanish   Eduardo E. Arriaga, Center for International Research, U.S. Bureau of the Census, Washington, D.C.

Italian   Emilio Casetti, Department of Geography, Ohio State University, Columbus, Ohio
Massimo Livi Bacci, University of Florence, Florence, Italy

German   Hilde Wander, Kiel Institute of World Economics, Kiel, West Germany (retired)

Japanese   Haruo Sagaza, Department of Sociology, Waseda University, Tokyo, Japan
Shigeru Kojima, formerly a sociologist at the University of California, Berkeley, Calif.; presently a professor in Tokyo

Chinese   Florence L. Yuan, Center for International Research, U.S. Bureau of the Census, Washington, D.C.
Wen-shun Chi, Center for Chinese Studies, University of California, Berkeley, Calif. (deceased)

Russian   Mikhael S. Bernstam, Fellow, Hoover Institution on War, Revolution, and Peace, Stanford, Calif.
Murray Feshbach, Center for Population Research, Georgetown University, Washington, D.C.
Hilja Kukk, Reference Librarian, Hoover Institution on War, Revolution, and Peace, Stanford, Calif.

About the Authors

WILLIAM PETERSEN is Robert Lazarus Professor of Social Demography Emeritus at Ohio State University. Among his books and longer monographs are *The Politics of Population, Japanese Americans: Oppression and Success, Population,* and *Malthus.* He has published some sixty papers in such journals as *Population and Development Review, Population Studies, Demography,* and *American Sociological Review,* as well as contributing to the *Harvard Encyclopedia of American Ethnic Groups* and *The Political Economy of National Statistics,* a monograph on the 1980 United States census.

RENEE PETERSEN was born in Vienna and educated in France, Italy, and Cuba. Her professional experience has been mainly in university administration, and she was the senior author of *University Adult Education: A Guide to Policy.* With the administrative skills she developed in her past positions and her facility in several languages, she was able to control the mass of materials from a thousand scattered sources that eventually were assembled in the five volumes of the *Dictionary of Demography.*